GET THE BEST
How to Recruit the People You Want

GET THE BEST

How to Recruit the People You Want

Catherine D. Fyock

This publication is designed to provide accurate and
authoritative information in regard to the subject matter
covered. It is sold with the understanding that neither the
author nor the publisher is engaged in rendering legal, accounting,
or other professional service. If legal advice or other expert
assistance is required, the services of a competent
professional person should be sought.

*From a Declaration of Principles jointly adopted by a Committee
of the American Bar Association and a Committee of Publishers.*

Library of Congress Cataloging-in-Publication Data

Fyock, Catherine D.
    Get the best : how to recruit the people you want / by Catherine
D. Fyock.
        p.   cm.
    ISBN 0-9661730-0-7
    1. Employees—United States—Recruiting. I. Title.
HF5549.5.R44F96   1993
    658.3'111—dc20   92–41384

Printed in the United States of America

  2 3 4 5 6 7 8 9

To the memory of Gary D. McCain;

His compassion and concern for others touched the lives

of many people.

Preface

Who's concerned with recruitment in this era of layoffs, right-sized organizations, and a recovering economy? Who needs to be looking at strategies for recruitment when there are still long unemployment lines?
  Consider these recent findings:

- The demand for college graduates will outpace supply for the rest of the 1990s, reports Cornell University's Center for Advanced Human Resource Studies.

- There is a tight supply of skilled, qualified employees that match the specific needs of businesses, causing a rise in salaries for skilled professional and technical positions, states *Human Resource Management News.*

- Employment activity is expected to rise significantly in the next months, according to a survey of 15,000 U.S. business firms conducted by Manpower Inc., with 25 percent of the firms noting an increase in staffing needs.

- Dun & Bradstreet's latest quarterly survey of 3,000 companies finds that 60 percent of executives predicted higher sales this fall, and the number of firms that planned to add workers nearly doubled from last winter, reports a *New York Times* article.

- A recent *Wall Street Journal* article finds that many businesses are experiencing increased hiring needs, including Audio Video Affiliates, adding 130 jobs at new stores; Bob Evans Farms hiring about 2,500 workers in 25 new stores; and Rite-Aid boosting drug-store employment 8 percent this year.

Many organizations have developed a blasé approach to recruitment: let the good candidates seek out employment opportunities. Until recently the employer with job openings has enjoyed a buyer's market. However, as the economy recovers and becomes healthier, as employers begin to add staff and replenish vacancies, and as employees who have been watching and waiting until the job market improves before making a move begin to seek out jobs that provide them with the satisfaction they want, more organizations will find that creative recruitment strategies are more important than ever before in identifying and wooing the best, most qualified candidates.

Get the Best is dedicated to all those recruiters, human resource professionals, business owners, and managers responsible for hiring good people for their organizations. It is intended to be a resource tool to provide you with ideas to use or to adapt to assist you in developing a better pool of qualified candidates from which to select your next employees.

This book focuses on how to attract and recruit the best employees, a subject that is often overlooked in many books and articles on recruitment and selection. Often, recruitment, or the attraction of qualified candidates, is given 10 percent of the time and attention, with information on selection given the remaining 90 percent of emphasis.

However, since organizations can only select those candidates who are first recruited to the organization, the primary step in having the best employees is to think more creatively and innovatively about the recruitment process.

Get the Best will give you literally hundreds of new ideas about how to attract top candidates cost-effectively. And, since "doing more with less" has become the corporate anthem for the 1990s, this book will provide you with ideas on attracting the best candidates with fewer budget dollars.

Many of the recruitment activities outlined in this book can be modified to meet your organization's specific staffing needs. For example, an open house sponsored by Compaq is outlined, in which the company spent $100,000 per recruitment event. In many cases, open houses can be conducted at a far less expense and still meet the organization's needs. Likewise, some employers have used television as a medium for recruitment advertising, using high-cost prime-time advertising, as well as no-cost or low-cost options, such as cable television and public service announcements. Therefore, recruiters will be made aware of the opportunities in tailoring recruitment activities to meet their own budget constraints.

For each chapter in the book, a matrix has been provided, which outlines some of these considerations, such as how targeted the activity can be, lead time, cost, and the number of people recruited through the activity. This can be used as an easy reference guide to identify key recruitment activity opportunities when staffing needs arise.

Chapter One introduces new ideas about how recruitment and staffing are different today and applies marketing and sales strategies to the recruitment function to increase the effectiveness of recruitment activities and messages. This chapter outlines ten principles of recruitment, providing you with new ways to rethink recruitment today.

Chapter Two talks about Workforce 2000, and the challenge of recruiting for diversity in the workplace. This chapter reviews different labor-market segments, such as women, older workers, persons with disabilities, minorities, and other special segments. For each labor-market segment, there is a discussion of some creative methods to target these groups through specific messages and activities.

Chapter Three provides some nontraditional and creative ways employers are trying today to find people. Notably, telemarketing (or telerecruiting), television, radio, direct mail, and other creative strategies will be presented.

Chapter Four takes a look at the geographic boundaries used for recruitment, and shares some innovative ways employers use to expand those traditional recruitment parameters.

Chapter Five covers newspaper advertising, one of the most commonly used recruitment strategies. This chapter highlights new ways to use newspaper advertising, including the use of different newspapers, alternate sections, different types of ads, and creative techniques for updating this traditional recruitment strategy.

Chapter Six reveals more updated ideas for the traditional recruitment activities, such as school recruiting, open houses, and career and job fairs. Chapter Seven outlines the role of image and retention in the recruitment strategy.

Chapter Eight concludes with a review of implementation guidelines, including tracking and documentation considerations, along with ideas for selling recruitment ideas to top management. An Appendix is provided that details recruitment sources to help you meet your goals.

As the economy recovers, employers will find that recruitment is again becoming a key strategic business activity that will determine if their organization can meet the challenges of high productivity, top quality and services, and a continued commitment to excellence.

Catherine D. Fyock

Contents

Introduction

R ecruitment is a challenge today—more so than it has been in the past. This was brought to light for me when I worked with Kentucky Fried Chicken Corporation (KFC) from 1983 until I left to begin my own business in 1987. I was director of field human resources, and had responsibility for about 5,000 employees in the southeastern United States.

KFC had always relied on a young work force and traditionally had no problems in recruiting the people it needed to staff its restaurants, especially with the baby boomer generation providing plenty of workers. However, in about 1985 we started to experience the beginning of the "baby bust," and in our growth markets of Atlanta, central Florida, and North Carolina, staffing became the number one priority in running the business.

Particularly in the central Florida markets of Tampa and Orlando, the business was facing dramatic challenges. We began to experience hourly employee turnover rates in excess of 250 percent, and management vacancy rates soared above 45 percent. In other words, over 45 percent of the management positions within those markets were unfilled because we could not attract and keep the right employees.

Needless to say, we were frantic. We knew we had to resolve the problems immediately, as the staffing issues were impacting our ability to do business. Further, we saw that the staffing problems were compounding themselves. For example, if a restaurant had high hourly turnover, it meant that the manager was spending an excessive amount of time recruiting and training new employees, and spending management time in filling in while the employee was being replaced and then while the new employee was learning the job. The managers were burning themselves out, working 60, 70, even 80 hours a week. Then one of the managers would quit, leaving the rest of the management team to work harder and longer hours. Eventually there wasn't enough time to adequately train new employees, thus causing new employees to become frustrated and quit. The

1

cycle went on and on, creating higher turnover and vacancy rates. We knew we had to break this cycle.

The only solution was to develop a complete program for recruiting and retaining employees. I met with the district training manager and the rest of the human resources and operations team from this market, and we brainstormed as to what kinds of strategies would work.

In these meetings, we decided to try a variety of strategies and activities—we were afraid to rely on one or two methods to pull us out of this staffing dilemma. We also wanted to attack the problem of staffing at both the hourly and management levels.

The ideas that we as a team developed are the framework for this book. One of the basic concepts we discussed was the need to look at different types of employee groups that we had traditionally not *targeted* for recruitment in the past—groups like older workers and persons with disabilities. We had already learned that these nontraditional workers were virtually untapped, and that there were some excellent opportunities for us in attracting these workers, based upon our previous (but limited) experiences.

We also felt that we could do a lot to update some of the more traditional recruitment strategies, like newspaper advertising, school recruiting, open houses, and career fairs. We also wanted to explore some brand-new ideas, such as telemarketing (or telerecruiting), television, radio, direct mail, and kiosk advertising. We thought there might also be possibilities in expanding the geographic boundaries from which we had recruited in the past, through relocation options, busing, and other creative transportation efforts.

Another key component of our strategy was to look at image and retention, and the role each played in recruitment and staffing. We developed attitude surveys, we initiated exit interview programs, and we reintroduced our managers to the basic good-management principles of listening, communicating, counseling, motivating, and rewarding employees.

We began to work more closely with our public relations departments in developing strategies for creating a more positive image as an employer, and we began to brainstorm with the marketing department for more creative ideas to market and sell to a new customer group—employees and prospective employees.

The great news was that the plan began to work! Within a six-month period, we had dramatically reduced escalating turnover rates and vacancy rates. The 250 percent hourly employee turnover rate was reduced to something below 200 percent (closer to the 180 percent turnover rate experienced by the quick-service restaurant industry at that time), and the management vacancy rates soaring to 45 percent were reduced to the norm of 2 percent.

It was about this time that I had the opportunity to speak at the Society for Human Resource Management's national conference, held in 1987 in Kansas City. I spoke on the topic of nontraditional methods for recruiting employees, speaking about my experience with KFC. Not only were both my sessions packed, but I was written up in seven trade and professional publications, which led me to believe that this was a topic that a lot of people wanted more information about.

In 1988, I struck out in business for myself, offering management consulting services on strategies for recruiting and retaining employees. In those years in business, I have continued to learn about some creative and imaginative successful recruitment strategies, activities, messages, and principles that I'll share with you in these pages.

This book is designed to help you to discover new ideas for making your recruitment efforts more successful, to help you understand what you need to do differently in recruitment today, and to outline the ''how to'' steps and guidelines for creating effective recruitment programs.

The recruitment strategies outlined here are in an easy-to-reference format, so that once you've read the book in its entirety, you can quickly go back to the book to find out about how to put on an open house, how to attract nontraditional workers, or how to put together a direct-mail campaign.

I strongly believe that recruitment today is one of the most exciting, challenging components of running a business, and will continue to be one of the top competitive issues for the 1990s and beyond. If we cannot attract and recruit top employees for our business, we are doomed to mediocrity and, ultimately, failure—because it is our employees who are the lifeblood of our organizations.

Chapter One

A Marketing Approach
to Recruitment

The combined impact of labor scarcity and the emergence of the new work force presents both challenge and opportunity.

America has the chance, for the first time, to make good on its commitment to opportunity. If companies are to meet their labor needs, they will have to broaden the ethnic and gender makeup of their work forces. In other words, "affirmative action" will no longer be primarily a matter of social responsibility or legal compulsion, but of economic necessity.

On the other hand, companies will be faced with the challenge that traditional forms of affirmative action will not be enough. Rather, if our nation's companies are to remain productive and competitive, they must go beyond traditional notions of affirmative action, moving aggressively to remove the practical impediments that prevent people, whatever their color or ethnicity or gender or disability, from taking full advantage of the employment opportunities now available. It means a substantial investment in human capital—the one type of capital that can set us apart from our world competitors.[1]

As seen in the above excerpt from *Opportunity 2000*, the 1988 report authored by the Hudson Institute, commissioned by the U.S. Department of Labor, there are tremendous staffing opportunities and challenges for organizations facing the future. One of the biggest opportunities for employers is for the recruitment of nontraditional labor-market segments to meet staffing needs; the corresponding challenge is for organizations to understand each of these labor groups significantly enough to integrate them, through effective recruitment and retention strategies, into the organization.

As stated by Fred Alvarez, Assistant Secretary of Labor from 1987 to 1989, at the 1990 national conference of the Personnel Management Association of Aztlan [a nonprofit, national organization of primarily, but not exclusively, Hispanic human resources (HR) professionals]:

Companies that will survive in the year 2000 will do these things right:

First, they won't let discrimination happen. As the work force diversifies, there will be more people who won't put up with it.

Second, they should hire imaginative human resource people who can use diversity in the work force to their advantage.

And third, they must treat their employees like customers—developing them and their loyalty.[2]

One of the biggest challenges for employers today is to expand their traditional recruiting strategies to tap the potential of this new and changing labor market. Creative and innovative ways that effectively target nontraditional labor-market segments can meet the revised staffing goals that include the realization of the opportunities of the Workforce 2000.

THE CHALLENGE OF FINDING THE "RIGHT" EMPLOYEES

Recruitment in the recent past often assumed that the "right" candidates— those with the requisite skills, experience, education, and abilities—were actively seeking job opportunities. Increasingly today, many of the candidates most sought after by employers are those candidates who are happily working somewhere else, and are not engaged in a job search. Using more aggressive and intrusive forms of recruitment activities becomes one of the solutions for reaching these candidates.

AIN'T IT AWFUL!

Talk with most any recruiter, and you'll hear that finding qualified candidates in light of changing staffing goals is difficult at best. What makes recruitment so challenging today? Hear from typical recruiters as they discuss their difficulties in finding the "right" employees for Workforce 2000.

From a small business owner: "We are very interested in attracting older workers and people with disabilities, but we're unsure of how to attract these workers."

From a hospital recruiter: "I am faced with greater competition for labor than I have ever seen before. Wages, benefits, and working conditions are highly competitive, and recruiters are promising job candidates the moon in order to meet their goals.''

From a retailer: ''Unfilled positions compound the staffing problem, because when positions can't be filled, employees left behind must then do the jobs of two people, causing burnout and eventually, more vacancies.''

From a technical recruiter: ''Candidates today don't seem to have the same skills and abilities as candidates in the past. Our organization has to interview many more applicants just to get one qualified hire.''

From a health care recruiter: ''It's hard to believe it, but in many cases the job candidates have actually begun to interview *me*!''

From a corporate recruiter: ''The lead time it takes to fill open positions is increasing. It used to take a few weeks to fill secretarial and clerical positions; now it can take up to three months.''

From a small business owner: ''I am finding that many candidates who are offered the job and accept often don't show up for their first day of work.''

A NEW MODEL FOR RECRUITMENT: MARKETING AND SALES

Many of the best organizations, committed to recruiting and attracting the best candidates, have been searching for a new model for approaching the recruitment function—a model that recognizes the changes of Workforce 2000 and the need for the right employee. One central theme in developing this new model is the concept of employees as customers. It makes sense: as job seekers, we shop for a variety of life experiences to meet our needs and expectations. We want challenge; we want opportunity; we want growth; we want happiness; we want the things that money can buy. We see all of these elements as the components of a job—the work environment and the terms and conditions of employment. All of these are products that we are willing to purchase, not with money, but with the exchange of ourselves. In this analogy, the job candidate becomes the potential customer, with the employee as the customer. Recruitment becomes marketing and sales; retention translates to customer service (see Figure 1–1).

One large corporation that has embraced this concept is the Marriott Corporation. In their attempt to be the best lodging and food service com-

FIGURE 1-1

Job = Product
Terms and conditions of employment = Product features
Employee = Customer
Recruitment = Marketing and sales
Retention = Customer service
Human resources = Marketing and customer service

---

pany in the world, they developed an integrated employee program, treating employees in ways that create an extraordinary work environment.

Marriott began the process by applying a marketing approach, thinking of employees as a new customer group. Just as they had conducted focus groups with customers to determine customer interests, needs, and motivations, they initiated similar focus groups with employees to determine which features of jobs would be appealing to different employee groups.

Marriott discovered with its Roy Rogers division (since sold to Hardee's Food Systems) that certain needs were common to all employee groups, including clear promotion guidelines, paid vacations, a clean work environment, good supervision, and respect for the employee. Beyond these common needs, however, there were four distinctive employee groups, with unique sets of needs and motivations for work.

One group, for example, was the ''pay-first'' group, which would work for the most competitive salaries. Another group desired the corporate climate of a large, prestigious hotel chain. Another group wanted, above all else, flexibility in work hours and schedules, while a fourth group wanted to work with Marriott because of their desire to work in fast-food management.

After identifying these four segments, Marriott then developed, through a marketing process, a profile of high-potential employees. They also made some decisions as to whether or not they would try to continue to attract all market segments, with the final decision to abandon efforts at targeting those in the pay-first category, understanding that some of these individuals would be in applicant pools and could still be selected for recruitment.

Through this process it became apparent that the job candidates motivated by food-service careers would respond to different messages and recruitment activities than the other groups, as would those in the flexible-hours group and the corporate-climate group. By using a marketing approach, Marriott determined that a variety of marketing, or recruiting, approaches were to be used to attract employees, as were a corresponding set of customer service, or retention strategies to keep those employees. As stated by Pam Farr, vice president of Human Resources Planning and Development for Marriott, "One size does not fit all!"

Other organizations realize the importance of applying marketing principles to recruitment, including NEC Information Systems, Inc. When NEC faced the need to improve their recruitment effectiveness, the corporation turned to marketing principles to guide their decisions.

NEC formed focus groups to evaluate the effectiveness of past advertising campaigns, and to develop concepts for future strategies. They selected focus group members from people employed in a marketing or systems analyst position, with two thirds employed by computer-related companies.

Respondents participated in surveys designed to assess how they went about looking for a job and what information was helpful. They also took part in a tachistoscope (T-scope) evaluation, in which ads were flashed in varying time lengths with respondents being asked to identify the advertising company. Then participants answered open-ended questions regarding various elements of the NEC advertising campaign.

As a result of the marketing research techniques, the organization was able to make significant changes in advertising design and message content, resulting in high-quality hires and a dramatic decrease in placement agency use, lowering cost-per-hire rates. The total exempt hires through advertising increased from 19 percent to 41 percent, and hires through agencies decreased from 47 percent to 10 percent. The decrease in agency use alone saved the company almost $500,000.[3]

Another company used a sales approach to meet extraordinary recruitment goals. National Liberty in Chester County, Pennsylvania, had 311 open positions to fill between January and April, in a county experiencing 2 percent unemployment. Their goal: to fill *all* 311 positions!

The entire human resource department became involved in the process, even though many of them had no prior training in the recruitment arena. They used a sales blitz approach, with meetings each morning for daily updates and brainstorming sessions. All members of the sales team wore special T-shirts and carried whistles, which were blown anytime a "sale" (hire) was made.

Members of the sales force distributed over 20,000 leaflets door-to-door, designed newspaper fliers, and participated in the selection process. The telemarketing staff joined in, contacting residents who had received the door-hanger recruitment messages.

The company awarded incentives if everyone met the goal for 100 percent filled positions, which they did. Prizes included a compact disc (CD) player, three-day cruises, and overnights at area bed-and-breakfasts. The sales program ended with an awards banquet, honoring those who had worked so hard throughout the campaign.[4]

IDEAS NO. 1–10: MARKETING PRINCIPLES FOR RECRUITMENT TODAY

Translating marketing concepts into recruitment actions is the top priority for those responsible for finding the best candidates today.

IDEA NO. 1: SELECT THE TARGET MARKET FOR RECRUITMENT EFFORTS, AND DEVELOP SPECIFIC MESSAGES AND ACTIVITIES TO REACH THAT AUDIENCE

McDonald's, one of the world's premier advertisers, would like to sell hamburgers to the world. Yet their approach to advertising has not been toward generic ads, but rather, to a targeted advertising approach. They have Ronald McDonald to appeal to the very young customers. They created the now-famous commercial of the older man working on his first day at McDonald's to appeal to the older customer. They have a variety of minorities depicted in commercials to appeal to minority customers.

This same targeted approach to recruitment marketing should be used when the targeted audience can be differentiated by needs, motivations, and concerns. Therefore, if you are interested in attracting minority candidates, then you need to develop specific, targeted recruitment messages for this market. Likewise, organizations wanting to target older workers for recruitment activities should develop activities and messages that speak to this market.

Targeting in recruitment can be accomplished in a number of ways. Testimonial ads are excellent, in that they depict a member of the targeted audience—either pictorially or in words—showing the targeted audience why your organization is a good employment choice. Testimonial ads can depict a labor-market segment, such as older workers, minorities, persons with disabilities, and women, or can depict occupations from which candidates might want to consider a job change. One line of advertising developed by a food-service employer, for example, showed individuals from other occupations and industries, such as secretarial, teaching, and health care, who had made the switch to the food-service industry and were happy about their choice. The testimonial is effective in advertising because it is most similar to one of the most effective advertising methods—word of mouth.

Another method to target recruitment efforts is to include pictures, either actual photographs or illustrations, of the targeted audience. Pictures can be used in newspaper advertising, recruitment brochures and literature, direct-mail pieces, posters, and television.

Targeting can also be accomplished by selecting media or activities that are particularly appealing to the target audience. For example, placing a recruitment message in *Black Collegian* will reach minority college students. Ads placed near the obituary section of the newspaper will tend to attract older workers. An open house held at a department store with information on job-search activities for reentering the work force will appeal to some women.

Recruitment messages can be targeted when the ad copy demonstrates that the needs of the targeted audience will be met, or when the copy appeals to a specific audience. For example, an ad stating that maturity, experience, and judgment are highly desired will send a message to older candidates. Copy emphasizing opportunities for advancement and growth will be particularly appealing to minorities and women. A message relaying that the organization provides flexible work schedules will attract students, older workers, and women, among others.

Is a targeted approach really needed? Many recruiters and hiring managers have concerns that a targeted approach will exclude many candidates because of this focus, diminishing the response rates. Actually, the opposite is true. A targeted approach permits the organization to clearly communicate to that audience that there is real interest in the targeted candidate. A generic approach ends up appealing to no one.

What about equal employment opportunity (EEO) guidelines? Can't a targeted approach be construed by some as discriminatory? Recruitment activities and messages should not imply that a member of a protected class is excluded from employment opportunities. And, unless there is a bona fide occupational qualification (BFOQ) for a limitation to one sex, for example, advertisements should not indicate a preference for or a limitation to one sex. Certain words and phrases should be excluded from advertising, such as *young*, *college student*, *recent college graduate*, *boy*, *girl*, or any specification for an age group.[5]

As long as your total recruitment activities are balanced on the whole, with activities and messages for all candidates without excluding any audience, then the targeted approach is entirely permissible. As stated by the College Placement Council Inc.'s general counsel, Rochelle K. Kaplan, targeted programs are legal as long as they are not "exclusive." Says Kaplan, "Targeted recruitment is permissible; exclusive recruitment is illegal."[6]

IDEA NO. 2: DEVELOP RECRUITMENT MESSAGES AND ACTIVITIES THAT SELL THE JOB OPPORTUNITY

Messages and activities that merely say "help wanted" are not very effective today, in that they fail to sell prospective candidates on why they should consider the job opportunity. Effective recruitment strategies show candidates what's in it for them, by appealing to their needs, concerns, and motivations for work. Like successful sales approaches, selling the job should include not just a description of the features of the job opportunity, but also the advantages and benefits of work.

Candidates want to know about benefits, salary, training and growth opportunities, advancement, the kind of work environment, corporate culture, rewards and recognition programs, and other specifics. Include as many as possible of these selling features, advantages, and benefits in your recruitment advertisements.

Advertisements should use selling techniques to make them appealing to candidates. Larger ads will tend to attract the eye, as will borders, graphics, white space, and bold type. See Chapter Five for additional information on designing ads to sell candidates.

Selling activities should go beyond the initial advertising campaign. One health care organization was having a difficult time getting candidates to accept offers of employment. Even though the human resources department was referring many qualified candidates to the hiring managers, the hiring managers were striking out with these candidates. In a study of this issue in a focus group, hiring managers were asked about how they sold the job opportunity to candidates. They looked at each other, quizzically shrugged their shoulders, and replied that they really didn't have anything special to offer candidates! No wonder this organization was having difficulties in getting hires! These managers desperately needed training on how to sell the job opportunity during the interviewing process.

IDEA NO. 3: MAKE IT EASY FOR JOB CANDIDATES—THE ELUSIVE CUSTOMERS—TO BUY

Many candidates today aren't actively seeking employment, especially during times of low unemployment and labor shortages. These candidates are similar to window shoppers in that they might consider a purchase decision if the right opportunity presented itself. Therefore, recruitment today needs to make it easy for the potential applicant to explore the employment opportunity with you.

To attract those candidates not actively seeking employment, a company must examine a more intrusive approach to recruitment. These are methods that reach out to job candidates during the course of their daily activities. Intrusive approaches include telemarketing and direct mail, as well as placement of advertising where candidates are not necessarily looking for employment, such as alternative sections of the newspaper (sports section, television section, or food section, for example).

Since these candidates are not actively seeking employment, the best recruitment activities avoid a quick close to the sale, but rather, invite candidates to explore the opportunities with you. Messages that invite candidates to send in for additional information (say, a recruitment brochure or information sheet) or call for more information are better than those asking for candidates to send in their résumé, or to apply in person. Open houses and career fairs are most attractive to candidates who are not yet ready to sign up for a more formal interview, but are interested in learning more about your organization.

The requirement for a résumé can be a discourager for candidates who don't have a current one prepared, and since many candidates are working elsewhere, this can be difficult. One candidate shared that although he was interested in a position with a certain employer, he was unable to get access to a typewriter or computer to update his résumé by the required deadline. It wasn't a priority for this candidate, so he didn't apply. This employer missed out on a qualified candidate because it was too difficult to explore the employment opportunity.

A better method is to include a clip-out coupon that a candidate can complete and mail in. The Army National Guard placed such an advertisement in *Time* magazine, with a coupon asking for name, address, phone, social security number, and educational level. The ad read, "I understand there is no obligation."

Wendy's International, Inc. based in Dublin, Ohio, uses a similar coupon, asking candidates to send in a résumé, or complete the coupon, which asks for name, address, phone, the best time to be reached, previous experience, and educational level.

One temporary help agency, Temp Associates in Irvine, California, uses a coupon ad to capture candidate contact information in addition to clerical skills, including the types of office equipment used, locations within the county most interested in working, and the days and times available for work. The ad also asks candidates if they are interested in learning more about the company's word processing training program.

Hyundai uses a caption for their clip-out ad stating, "The Great Career Rip-Off is at the bottom of this ad!" They list a number of different positions for which they are recruiting and ask candidates to send for more information by completing the basic contact information, along with job title interest.

Cole Vision Corporation, in a recruitment brochure, provides a perforated coupon for candidates to send in, along with a toll-free 800 number for interested individuals to call for additional information.

Many employers are using employment hot lines so that interested candidates can call and receive a recorded message on job openings. The cost can be relatively low; the only items necessary are a dedicated phone line and an answering machine.

Other employers are merely being available during Sundays, when most employment advertisements are run, to answer the phone regarding employment inquiries. This approach permits employers to take advantage of that "impulse buy" of the candidate who is just window shopping. Employers are also opening their employment offices on evenings and weekends to attract qualified candidates.

Toll-free 800 numbers are another approach gaining in popularity for employers seeking candidates from a broad geographic area. Employers can either administer this service in-house, or use the services of a variety of companies who provide this service for a fee. Some of the larger recruitment advertising agencies provide these services to their clients for a fee.

Most toll-free services operate by charging the employer a minimum monthly fee, with a fee-per-call. The fee-per-call is usually determined by how many questions are asked of the candidate, and the nature of the question (disqualifying questions, open or closed questions, for example). Employers can retrieve data via fax, first-class mail, United Parcel Service (UPS) next day, or via a computer dial-up, download feature. Costs are also based upon the retrieval method used.

Employers can use toll-free numbers merely to elicit response from candidates or to sign up candidates for attendance at recruitment events, such as open houses or information seminars. One employer uses an 800-number advertisement to ask candidates to call in for more details regarding their upcoming open house, and another toll-free ad to entice burned-out candidates to call in for more information, with the headline, "Take two aspirins & call us in the morning."

IDEA NO. 4: ROLL OUT THE RED CARPET FOR PROSPECTIVE JOB CANDIDATES

Since prospective employees are a potential internal customer, employers need to develop ways to make the candidate feel welcomed throughout the employment process. One friend shared a recent experience in being interviewed for a middle-management job: The human resources department kept her waiting for 20 minutes, then interviewed her hastily. Then after waiting for 45 minutes for the hiring manager (he forgot she was waiting), she was asked to reschedule her appointment because the hiring manager was called into another meeting. This friend concluded that she didn't want to work for any company that had so little regard for a job applicant; she believed that she would be treated no better as an employee.

An employer's first chance at creating a positive image with that job candidate is in the employment process. Evaluate your organization's response to candidates in each of these processes.

- How are candidates first greeted when they call in for an appointment? Are they treated with respect and dignity? Many receptionists and department secretaries are used to the treatment often given to baby boomer candidates: since so many of them wanted the job very badly, any treatment was acceptable because the ones who wanted the jobs most would get them. The philosophy then was, "Don't call us; we'll call you."

- Are candidates greeted with warmth when they appear for the job interview? Those responsible for this greeting should show warmth and hospitality. Offer the candidate a beverage; offer to take the candidate's coat. Inform those applying about the time schedule for the employment process.

- Have you prepared for the interview—both the job site and your mind-set—prior to the interview?

- Are all interviewers trained in the interviewing process? Do they understand how to conduct a thorough screening interview?

- Have you assigned a "host" when you have multiple interviews scheduled for the interview in order to make the candidate more comfortable?

- Do you keep applicants waiting, or are they escorted quickly from one interview to the next? Again, prompt attention demonstrates regard for the individual's time, an important customer service element.

- How do candidates learn about the status of their résumé or application, or the status of the search process? Do you acknowledge receipt of résumés and applications? Are candidates kept informed as to when a decision will be made? Some employers, in conjunction with a résumé tracking database program, are able to respond promptly to candidates' résumés or applications. If you don't have such a software program, you can keep applicant correspondence stored in your word processing programs and keep in touch with candidates regularly.

One way to test your organization to see how well you respond to job candidates is to do what Walt Disney World does in Lake Buena Vista, Florida. Disney, committed to excellence in customer service, has always used mystery shoppers (external contractors posing as customers) to test the quality of services received. Disney has also tested the quality of services received by internal customers, and has hired mystery shoppers who pose as job applicants to evaluate the employment process.

One retailer recently shared that his company began a similar process, only to be horrified at the results. Candidates were treated rudely, made to wait long periods of time, and failed to receive appropriate follow-up on employment inquiries. Another manager reported that she decided to test how competitors treated job applicants and posed as a candidate asking for a job. She was delighted to find out that the competition mistreated candidates badly—giving her company a distinct advantage!

IDEA NO. 5: CREATE A POSITIVE RECRUITMENT IMAGE

What do your recruitment activities and messages say about you as an employer? Are you communicating what you intend?

Take the example of the homebuyer who is looking for that new home in the multiple listings book. For the would-be buyer who sees the same home in the book week after week, the question arises, "What's wrong with that home? What does someone else know that I don't know?"

This is also true for the employer with the same advertisement running week after week. The job candidate begins to wonder, "What's wrong with that employer? Why can't they fill their open positions? Can't they keep good employees?" A better process is to limit the number of advertisements running in the same place, targeted to the same audience, with the same message. Vary the types of recruitment mediums, using newspaper along with television, direct mail, magazines, school recruitment, radio, and posters, for examples. Vary the messages, with different ad copy appealing to retirees, college students, and work-force reentrants (without excluding any group in the process).

Another way to create that positive image is to pay attention to the words you use in your ads. One employer found that they were receiving no response when a readerboard said, "Help Wanted." An ingenious recruiter changed the readerboard message to say, "Place your name on our recruitment waiting list," and found that before long the organization had a long list of qualified, eager applicants.

Work with your public relations department, if you have one, to develop positive-image campaigns within your community. One human resource manager was amazed to find how helpful her public affairs department was in developing news releases focusing on employment issues, and in creating programs designed to heighten public awareness of the organization as a great place to work. She was also surprised to find this department having budget funds available for human resources projects!

IDEA NO. 6: COLLABORATE WITH OTHERS TO ACHIEVE RECRUITMENT GOALS

Recruiters know that they can do their best work when there are others in the community to rely on as their recruiting partners. One recruiter reported that he had worked very hard with government agencies and community colleges and vocational schools in the area and had made many friends there who were always looking for candidates to refer to him.

Your goal as a recruiter is to build relationships with others who will share your commitment to find the best candidates for your organization—to become the "preferred employer" with schools, clubs and organizations, agencies, programs, and even other employers.

How can you become the preferred employer? It doesn't happen overnight. It takes the building of relationships over time. Get to know the placement professionals who can provide the most help to your organization. Visit them in their offices and understand how they operate. Invite them to tour your facility. Provide them with lots of information on your organization, the positions for which you recruit, and the advantages and benefits of working with your organization. Provide them with feedback on candidates they refer. Thank them for their efforts. All of these activities lead to the development of that preferred employer status that is earned over time.

Employers can work together to solve unique recruitment issues that would be virtually impossible to resolve independently. In several communities, employers have banded together to petition their department of transportation to provide much-needed public transportation to their area, so that job candidates from the inner city could reach the employment opportunities in their suburban location. Other employer groups have even gone together to provide transportation to employees.

Employers can work together in developing joint recruitment activities, such as career and job fairs and information seminars. Some complementary employers have shared recruitment advertising. Several subsidiary companies sharing a common parent company have formed alliances for recruitment activities.

When there is a recruitment activity you'd like to try but don't have the budget, time, resources, or expertise, ask yourself the question, "Whom can I work with to accomplish this goal?" Perhaps you can develop an alliance with a recruitment partner to achieve your objectives.

IDEA NO. 7: RECOGNIZE THAT RECRUITMENT IS A KEY SURVIVAL ISSUE IN BUSINESS TODAY

There is a story about two employers who went on a safari and became separated from their group. Before long, they found themselves face-to-face with a lion. One of the employers slowly bent down to pull a pair of sneakers from the backpack. The other employer said, "You must be crazy . . . you can't outrun that lion," to which the first employer responded, "I don't have to outrun the lion; I just have to outrun you!" And so it is with recruitment and staffing today: it is the key competitive, survival issue for the decade. If you can't recruit the best employees for positions within your organization, then the competition will.

Employers today must recognize their competitive strengths for labor. You should ask yourself, "How is my company better than my competition for labor?" Realize, too, that the question is about your competition for labor, not just your competitors for the products and services your organization offers. Thus, an employer seeking entry-level, unskilled workers may have as a labor competitor companies as varied as financial services, food service, insurance, health care, manufacturing, and retail.

What is your competitive advantage? Do you offer the best training program in the industry? The best starting wages? The most impressive opportunities for advancement? The most flexible schedules? The most secure employment? The best team atmosphere? Consider these and other elements, and use these competitive strengths in your recruitment strategy.

IDEA NO. 8: AVOID THE "TRIED AND TRUE" RECRUITMENT METHODS THAT ARE NO LONGER EFFECTIVE

Just because newspaper advertising, recruitment agencies, or other traditional methods have been used in the past doesn't necessarily mean that these methods should be used again to meet recruitment goals. Consider what is working for you today, and abandon or update those methods that are no longer "tried and true." In fact, what many recruiters are learning is that some of the most unusual, unique, and different approaches are the ones most effective today.

Recruiters should look to marketing principles and concepts to find out what makes sense to attract the best candidates. Just as many human resources professionals have met with their public affairs department to gain guidance on image campaigns, human resources and marketing departments are forming partnerships within organizations to design effective recruitment marketing programs. In the Marriott program reviewed earlier, human resources departments worked closely with marketing professionals to develop the strategies used in that successful program.

Employers can also learn from the "streetfighting" philosophies of marketing. Jeff Slutsky, a marketing consultant who calls himself "The Streetfighter," talks about how an upscale salon fought the competition when a budget salon moved in across the street. The budget salon purchased billboard space, claiming "$6 Haircuts." The upscale salon didn't want to budge on price or on their upscale image, so instead chose to capitalize on their image with a similar billboard which boasted, "We fix $6 haircuts." Consider what your unique marketing opportunity is in selling the features, advantages, and benefits of the employment experience, and use that in creating new recruitment strategies.

IDEA NO. 9: TRY A VARIETY OF RECRUITMENT MESSAGES AND ACTIVITIES TO REACH DIVERSE LABOR-MARKET SEGMENTS

Wouldn't it be wonderful if you were to read this book and discover a heading that said, "Here is the one perfect recruitment strategy that will solve all your problems." Unfortunately, there is no such animal.

Therefore, to be effective, recruitment strategies should incorporate a number of different messages and activities that will sufficiently reach the diversity of the workplace today. Remember the advice of the adage "Don't put all your eggs in one basket." Instead, look for new and unique ways to vary the medium, the activity, and the recruitment message. Carefully study the targeted audience, and look for specific ways to reach that audience.[7]

IDEA NO. 10: DEVELOP A STRATEGIC RECRUITMENT ACTION PLAN

As finding qualified candidates becomes more difficult, it becomes imperative for those responsible for recruitment to develop a complete recruitment-action plan. The first phase of this plan is in identifying the target market and in learning about ways in which this group can be reached. Next is the development of critical recruitment activities. Activities can be entirely new, nontraditional methods or they can be updated streetfighting approaches. Recruiters should review image issues to ensure that strategies are consistent, positive, and set realistic expectations. They should also analyze retention strategies and retention records, since a positive work environment and reputation are some of the best recruitment strategies possible. Finally, they should review the recruitment messages to ensure that the recruitment campaign is consistent, positive, and adequately meets the needs of prospective employees.

CONSIDERATIONS IN PLANNING FOR RECRUITMENT ACTIVITIES

Not every recruitment activity or strategy will yield the same results with the same level of time, money, staff, and other resources. Therefore, recruiters will need to carefully consider which plans make the most sense for inclusion in the overall staffing plan.

Some considerations that should be made by recruiters include the following:

- Cost of the activity and budget constraints.
- Ease of delivery.
- Lead time for implementing the activity.
- Resources involved (for example, the number of staff members needed to execute a successful open house).
- Availability of other resources for assistance (such as recruitment advertising agencies, search firms, and other third-party resources).

- Approvals necessary.
- Consistency with image, reputation, philosophy, and corporate culture.
- How the activity and message will be perceived by candidates.
- How the activity and message will be perceived by current employees.
- Effectiveness of recruitment activity and message in the past (as measured by various tracking mechanisms—refer to Chapter Eight for more information).

Recruiters should carefully evaluate these issues in deciding whether or not to implement various elements of the recruitment strategy. For example, if they need to fill three positions as soon as possible, some recruitment activities, such as initiating a college recruitment program or developing recruitment literature, may not be feasible because of these time limitations. Or, if there is only a small budget for recruitment, then some activities will need to be redesigned to fit into these constraints.

Ideas for a Marketing Approach to Recruitment

Idea No. 1: Select the target market for recruitment efforts, and develop specific messages and activities to reach that audience.

Idea No. 2: Develop recruitment messages and activities that sell the job opportunity.

Idea No. 3: Make it easy for job candidates—the elusive customers—to buy.

Idea No. 4: Roll out the red carpet for prospective job candidates.

Idea No. 5: Create a positive recruitment image.

Idea No. 6: Collaborate with others to achieve recruitment goals.

Idea No. 7: Recognize that recruitment is a key survival issue in business today.

Idea No. 8: Avoid the "tried and true" recruitment methods that are no longer effective.

Idea No. 9: Try a variety of recruitment messages and activities to reach diverse labor-market segments.

Idea No. 10: Develop a strategic recruitment action plan.

Ideas for a Marketing Approach to Recruitment

Idea	Cost	Number People	Lead Time	Target
Idea No. 1: Select target market	L	—	S–L	Y
Idea No. 2: Develop activities	L	—	S–L	Y
Idea No. 3: Make it easy to "buy"	L	—	S–L	N
Idea No. 4: Roll out the red carpet	L	—	S–L	N
Idea No. 5: Create positive image	L–H	—	S–L	Y
Idea No. 6: Collaborate with others	L	—	M–L	Y
Idea No. 7: Recognize key issue	L	—	S–L	Y
Idea No. 8: Avoid old methods	L–H	—	S–L	Y
Idea No. 9: Try variety of messages	L–H	—	S–L	Y
Idea No. 10: Develop action plan	L–H	—	M–L	Y

Key:

Cost		Lead time	
Low	0–$200	Short	0–1 week
Medium	$200–$1,000	Moderate	1 week–4 weeks
High	$1,000 +	Long	4 + weeks
Number people		Target	
Single	1	Yes	
Multiple	2 or more	No	
Either			

ENDNOTES

1. The Hudson Institute, *Opportunity 2000* (U.S. Department of Labor, 1988), p. 16.

2. Tammy Brecht-Dunbar, "Diverse Work Force Will End Discrimination," *HRNews*, March 1990, p. 11.

3. Albert H. McCarthy, "Recruitment," *Personnel Journal*, August 1989, pp. 84–87.

4. Connie Dorval, "Recruiting Campaign Gives New Meaning to 'Whistle Blower'," *Capital Holding Report*, July 1990, pp. 12–13.

5. Gerard P. Panaro, *Employment Law Manual* (Boston: Warren, Gorham & Lamont, 1990), pp. 1-2–1-4.

6. "Recruiters Face Mixed Directives," *The Fact Finder*, p. 2.

7. Catherine D. Fyock, *America's Work Force Is Coming of Age: What Every Business Needs to Know to Recruit, Train, Manage, and Retain an Aging Work Force* (Lexington, Mass.: Lexington Books, 1990), pp. 57–61.

Chapter Two

Recruiting the Workforce 2000

T he work force is changing, and in meeting employer goals, the new questions facing employers are as follows:

- What are the nontraditional labor-market segments that can be attracted to meet increasingly challenging staffing goals?

- What are the needs, motivations, and issues facing these nontraditional employees/customers so that their needs can be met in the staffing process?

- How can employers develop creative, innovative marketing-focused strategies that will attract these workers?

This chapter will investigate each of these questions, focusing each section on a specific labor-market segment, with identification of the issues impacting recruitment strategies, as well as a review of successful messages and activities that will appeal to each of these labor-market segments.

Before beginning, however, here is a word about identifying employee groups' characteristics and how this fits in with the diversity issue. While identifying common goals, needs, issues, and motivations for work of each of these various labor-market segments, remember that within these groups are individuals—individuals with unique goals, needs, issues, and motivations that may be quite dissimilar to those representative of the labor market as a whole. What all recruiters will need to appreciate is that while many of these concepts are identified as appropriate for attracting a labor-market segment as a whole, they will not always be appropriate given individual differences.

IDEA NO. 11: RECRUITING OLDER WORKERS

Recruitment Issues

While many employers are interested in targeting and attracting older workers for a wide variety of positions, employers are often finding that this is a difficult group to attract. One reason for this is that many older adults are not actively seeking employment. In fact, according to a survey conducted by the American Association of Retired Persons, only about 2 percent of the older adults that were questioned stated they were unemployed. Forty-eight percent did consider themselves to be retired; thirty-seven percent were already working in some capacity; twelve percent consider themselves to be homemakers. (See Figure 2–1.)

Greg Newton, president of Newton & Associates in Boston, Massachusetts, states that the large number of retirees and homemakers does not necessarily indicate a lack of interest in returning to the workplace, but rather an indication of traditional values. As many as one out of three retirees would consider a return to the workplace for the right opportunity.[1]

Recruiters need to realize that most older adults are not actively seeking employment, but would consider the right work situation if it was presented. Therefore, intrusive recruitment-advertising strategies will be most helpful in appealing to this market.

According to a variety of marketing studies of older adults, this labor market segment is highly diverse—more so than any other market segment. In several instances, including the Geromarket® study and the Lifestyles and Values of Older Adults study, reports show that there are at least six distinct market segments with unique and distinctive needs, values, and motivations for work.

At a management training program, one human resource professional asked the question about older adults. "I don't exactly understand what the profile is of the typical older adult. Is it the person who has retired with a healthy pension and is looking for work as a means to have fun, network with others, and feel productive? Or is it the person who is unable to find employment, has few skills, and needs competitive salary and benefits in order to get by?" The answer is, *both* are profiles of typical older adults.

The recruiter seeking to attract older adults should realize the diversity in this population, and design messages and activities that will appeal to a

FIGURE 2–1
Self-Perception of Work Status by Persons Aged 55+

Retired	48%
Work full-time	26
Homemaker	12
Work part-time	11
Unemployed	2
Disabled	2

Source: American Association of Retired Persons.

number of lifestyles, values, and motivations for work. Strategies might appeal to these needs:

- Financial security with competitive salary and benefits.
- Affiliation and the need to be with others.
- Feelings of being productive and making a contribution.
- Challenge the mind.
- Helping others.

Older adults also identify with different terms, depending upon their age. For example, individuals aged 55 would never be called senior citizens (in fact, many would be offended if you used that term!). Correspondingly, those aged 65 would not respond to the term *elderly*. (See Figure 2–2.)

Those involved with recruiting older adults should be aware of these differences and should take care in using terms that have the effect of tar-

FIGURE 2–2
Age and Identification Affiliation

Mature workers/adults	50–65
Retired	55–70
Older adults	55–70
Older workers	60–75
Seniors/senior citizens	65–80+
Golden agers	75–80+
Elderly	75–80+

Source: Catherine D. Fyock, *America's Work Force Is Coming of Age,* (Lexington, Mass.: Lexington Books, 1990).

geting in or out various labor-market segments. One employer, for example, attempting to recruit older adults ages 50 and older used the term *seniors* in recruitment-advertising copy, discouraging those younger-older workers aged 50 to 65.

Also be aware of the effect of pictures on recruiting older adults. Studies have shown that older adults tend to identify with pictures of people who are 7 to 15 years younger than they are, confirming the quote of Bernard M. Baruch, who said, "To me, old age is 15 years older than I am."

One employer found out how true this was when they developed targeted recruitment advertising for older adults. The ad depicted an illustration of an older man, who looked to be at least 80 years old. The ad didn't work, and it was no wonder—with the research study in mind, they were targeting a candidate aged 87 to 95!

One other issue in the recruitment of older adults is the desire for alternate work schedules. Often, the options afforded older workers are to continue working full-time or to retire. Increasingly, older adults are interested in reduced work schedules and in alternative work options. For example, many older workers are interested in part-time options, job sharing, telecommuting, and consulting arrangements. By offering alternatives, an employer can attract and retain older workers in the workplace. More information on staffing alternatives is outlined in Chapter Eight.

Targeted Recruitment Activities

Older adults are more likely to participate in recruitment activities that are targeted to them. Many older adults respond only to targeted activities because they have seen, only too clearly, that age discrimination is still very real today.

What kinds of activities tend to appeal to older adults? Consider the following:

- Conduct information seminars focusing on retirement issues, including financial information, health and fitness, and second and third career options.
- Hold open houses and career fairs especially for older adults, perhaps sponsored by an older worker organization in your community, such as the American Association of Retired Persons, the National Council on the Aging, or by your state's office on aging.
- Use targeted recruitment newspaper advertising, including advertising in alternate sections of the newspaper—the lifestyles section,

television section, and even the obituary section (older adults read this each day!).

- Hang posters in places that older adults frequent, such as health centers, senior centers, doctors' offices, banks, post offices, grocery stores, laundromats, and churches and community centers.

- Place messages in bargain shopper papers frequently read by older adults on fixed incomes—papers such as *Bargain Mart, Penny Pincher,* and *Thrifty Nickel.*

- Send direct-mail messages to older adults by using age selects to segment the audience receiving the mailer.

- Older worker organizations may be interested in cosponsoring recruitment activities. Contact these organizations to see how you might work together to meet your employment needs (refer to the Appendix for a detailed listing of organizations).

- Older worker task forces are an excellent method to find more older workers if your organization already has older adults within the work force. Ask older employees for referrals, as well as for specific ideas for attracting more experienced workers.

- Radio and television can be very targeted by gaining listener/viewer demographics from the local station. Look for low-cost spots with high concentrations of the population you want to attract.

- "Unretirement parties" have been a successful strategy used by companies like The Travelers, based in Hartford, Connecticut. They have effectively advertised these "parties" first with their own retirees, then with other retirees in the community to build a pool of part-time workers to meet temporary help needs.

- Invite your own retirees back to work through a targeted mailing, telephone call, or notice in your retiree newsletter.[2]

Targeted Recruitment Messages

Appeal to older adults by showing them that your organization understands their needs and concerns. Hardee's Food Systems, based in Rocky Mount, North Carolina, uses a series of targeted ads that let older adults know they are wanted. Ads featured include:

- "Tired of being retired?" (depicting a bored-looking older man with golf bag in tow).

- "How to ease back into the labor pool" (depicting a mid-aged woman peering off the end of a diving board).

- "Social Security leave you socially insecure?"
- "Relish your retirement years" (depicting a Hardee's hamburger).

You can also target advertisements by using words with which the older reader identifies. The words *mature, experienced,* and *reliable* will let older readers know you value what they have to offer.

Messages can also be targeted through the use of pictures. Some organizations are combining pictures with testimonials from older employees talking about the benefits of work with the company. Again, be aware of the inadvertent targeting that may occur with pictures. Initially, one business, in their attempts to target this market, selected obviously older models for recruitment. Later, the organization learned about this mistake in targeting the advertising too old to attract a sufficient number of interested candidates.

Be sure to include pictures of older adults in all recruitment literature. Check posters, brochures, advertisements, commercials, and other messages that depict employees and prospective employees. Make sure you are sending out the desired message.

Some employers are ensuring that older workers get the message about their interest by developing a program specifically for the increased employment of this market segment. Companies such as Hardee's Food Systems, McDonald's, and Kentucky Fried Chicken—fast-food employers aggressively seeking older, more experienced workers to replace the shortfall of younger workers traditionally targeted—have developed recruitment and retention programs for older workers, "New Horizons," "McMasters," and "The Colonel's Tradition," respectively. Kelly, the national temporary help agency based in Troy, Michigan, has initiated "Encore," a special program to attract older workers. Each of these programs has special recruitment literature to correspond to its theme of older-worker opportunities.

IDEA NO. 12: ATTRACTING PERSONS WITH DISABILITIES

Recruitment Issues

With the passage of the Americans with Disabilities Act (ADA), many employers will be increasingly interested in targeting people with disabilities for employment opportunities. This labor-market segment is one of the largest available to employers, with some 43 million people in the United States with some sort of physical or mental impairment. Further, this group has the highest unemployment rate—nearly 66 percent—representing an underutilized labor-market segment ready to be tapped by employers.

Perhaps the biggest obstacle to the increased employment of people with disabilities is the mind-set of managers who are unsure how these individuals can be utilized in the workplace. Many companies are developing sensitivity-training programs as part of a valuing diversity initiative to help managers overcome stereotypical thinking about people with disabilities.

Employers have a wonderful resource to assist them in making successful placements, in the form of rehabilitation professionals, counselors, and program directors. These professionals can be found in vocational rehabilitation programs, agencies, rehabilitation facilities, and state and local rehabilitation programs.

Another major hurdle to the increased employment of persons with disabilities is an understanding of job accommodation. Under ADA, reasonable accommodation must be made if the person is qualified to perform the essential job functions. Accommodation may take the form of modification to existing facilities, job restructuring, changing work schedules, purchasing or modifying equipment, adjusting or modifying training, or providing interpreters. Reasonable accommodation may not be required if the accommodation causes undue hardship on the employer, due to the nature and cost of the accommodation, the size, type, and financial resources of the facility. Considerations for undue hardship will include a review of the type of operation, makeup of the work force, and geographic issues.

Most accommodations are relatively inexpensive to make. A review of Figure 2–3 shows that according to the Job Accommodation Network, 50 percent of all job accommodations cost less than $50.[3]

A number of resources for job accommodation information are available to employers. Most notable is the Job Accommodation Network (JAN), which offers information and resources to employers interested in making job accommodation. A free service of the President's Committee on the Employment of Persons with Disabilities, they can be contacted via their toll-free 800 number (refer to the Appendix for details).

This service maintains a database of job accommodations made, and will permit interested employers to utilize this information given one caveat: that they share successful job-placement information with the network in order to perpetuate and update the service.

FIGURE 2–3
Cost of Job Accommodations

No cost	31%
$1–$50	19
$50–$500	19
$500–$1,000	19
$1,000–$5,000	11
$5,000+	1

Source: Michelle Neely Martinez, "Creative Ways to Employ People with Disabilities," *HRMagazine*, November 1990.

Another hurdle to successful placement of persons with disabilities is knowing the correct terminology to use. Many recruiters may even feel intimidated in not knowing the correct words in referring to disabilities or to persons with disabilities.

The current thinking on "correct" terminology is what's called "people first" language, which concentrates on the person first, then the disability. Thus the term *people with disabilities* is used instead of *disabled people*. Also, the term *disability* is preferred over *handicap*, since the original derivation of the term is literally "cap in hand"—begging for a wage. Other preferred terminology includes:

- "Nondisabled employees," not "regular employees."
- "Persons using a wheelchair," not "confined to a wheelchair."
- "Mentally disabled," not "retarded."
- "Vision and hearing impaired," not "deaf mute" or "deaf and dumb."
- "Disabled," not "afflicted" or "victim."

Targeted Recruitment Activities

Work closely with local and state vocational rehabilitation agencies that can provide your organization with job coaches and counselors who understand the capabilities of people with disabilities. These professionals can provide a number of valuable services, including:

- Analysis of the job description to determine essential job functions.
- Specific placement recommendations that match the capabilities of the individual with a disability.

- Analysis of what, if any, job accommodation is necessary.
- Provision of tips, guidelines, and how-to information on specific job accommodation processes (sometimes even the provision of the accommodation itself).

Work with your rehabilitation professional to determine what services you will need for your search, and what services the program will be able to provide. Give your resource person feedback so that a successful placement is easier to make.

In addition to assistance with placements, many rehabilitation programs offer supported employment services. In this situation, the rehab program has on staff a job coach, whose job it is first to learn the specific job tasks, then to work directly with the disabled employee to provide one-on-one training. There are tremendous advantages to the employer, in that, with the help of the job coach, there is one fully productive employee doing the job. As the new employee learns the job, the job coach phases out until services are no longer needed.

The job coach can also return to the job site if additional training is needed, if there are performance problems, or if the job substantially changes and retraining is necessary.

A job coach can work with single placements, or can work with multiple placements in an "enclave" setting. In an enclave, one job coach helps train several persons with disabilities at one time, usually in one location. Once the new employees are fully trained, they are then directed to their specific employment locale.

Avoid one of the hiring pitfalls commonly made by recruiters working with organizations providing services to persons with disabilities. The "multiple hire thinking trap" occurs when a recruiter, faced with many vacant positions, approaches the rehabilitation professional with the idea that all the staffing woes can be solved by placing many people with disabilities within the organization. Rehab professionals can perceive this as "warm body hiring," and may feel that this approach will be counter to their goals of a quality work life for their clients.

Instead, let rehabilitation professionals know you are interested in the quality of the work life of their clients, and want a successful placement. Make your goal "one successful placement at a time," and see if you don't get better responses from the programs with which you are working.

There are other methods to recruit persons with disabilities in addition to the use of agencies and programs. The Bank of Montreal wanted to demonstrate its commitment to employment equity with a new recruitment brochure. The collateral piece, ''Our Commitment to Opportunities'' depicted different ethnic groups in the cover illustration, and contained a blue braille message. The braille dots were actually drops of ink, which eliminated any distortion on the back of the recruitment piece.

The brochure was distributed to career counselors at the Canadian Paraplegic Association and the National Institute for the Blind, among other places. Stephen Cobbold, manager of recruitment, plans to develop another recruitment piece printed in large-size type, and another recorded on audiotapes. The commitment is also communicated to visually impaired customers with braille business cards.[4]

Consider these activities to attract persons with disabilities:

- Sponsor a career or job fair with a rehab agency or program to make opportunities available to persons with disabilities.
- Work with your local college, vocational school, or high school to attract students with disabilities.
- Develop joint recruitment activities, including posters, information seminars, or open houses with a rehabilitation program.
- Initiate a direct-mail campaign targeted to people with disabilities.
- Create a recruitment video and other collateral materials for teachers, counselors, and parents of people with disabilities. These are often the ''influencers'' who must be sold on the employment opportunity.
- Develop targeted recruitment advertising to place in newsletters, newspapers, magazines, and other publications with readership of persons with disabilities and of rehabilitation professionals.
- Develop a task force of employees with disabilities to help you discover ways to recruit more good employees.

Targeted Recruitment Messages

Recruitment messages must let people with disabilities know you are interested in them for employment. Messages can be direct in their appeal, or more subtle.

The example above of the Bank of Montreal shows a more direct approach. An advertisement by Philip Morris Companies Inc. in *Time* magazine demonstrates a more subtle approach, relying on the establishment of an image and reputation. The ad placed by Philip Morris was not a direct recruitment piece, but an image campaign centered around their support of the National Archives' celebration of the 200th anniversary of the Bill of Rights. It featured hearing-impaired actress Marlee Matlin with the testimonial, "For people like me the Bill of Rights is loud and clear."

The ad copy that follows is also a quote from Matlin:

> Hearing-impaired people have the same rights and privileges as anyone else in this society and that includes the right of access to information. That's why I've been such a strong proponent of closed captioning and signing whenever possible—movies, plays, TV. Without it, you have what amounts to a form of censorship.
>
> The Bill of Rights is the best defense against this kind of injustice.
>
> The hearing impaired can do anything anybody else can do. Look around you—there are deaf lawyers, deaf businessmen, deaf teachers, deaf actors—nothing impairs our creativity. Nothing.

While this is not a direct recruitment piece, it certainly gives a strong message to the hearing impaired, as well as other people with disabilities: Philip Morris is definitely an advocate for people with disabilities. And what a strong statement that is for recruitment purposes.

A similar recruitment message is sent indirectly by Citizens Fidelity Bank in Louisville, Kentucky. In an advertisement in the weekly business paper, *Business First,* the bank shows a large photograph of a Special Olympics winner crossing the finish line, with the headline, "We've funded some pretty amazing breakthroughs." The ad goes on to discuss their sponsorship of the Special Olympics games. Again, this advertisement is not a direct recruitment piece, but the message it sends about the support of people with disabilities will position this organization well with this labor-market segment.

Showing people with disabilities in all recruitment literature is another method to send the recruitment message to this population. Remember, too, that not all people with disabilities use wheelchairs, so use people with different types of disabilities in visual messages, including posters, recruitment brochures, television commercials, recruitment advertisements, and direct-mail messages.

Beware of one unfortunate practice that is taking place across the country: someone calls your company, usually the human resource professional or recruiter, claiming to be a representative of a magazine for people with disabilities (in similar scams, callers say that they represent other minority groups—disabled veterans, black Americans, etc.). The caller may say something like, "I just spoke with your chief executive officer (CEO), and I know how dedicated your organization is to people with disabilities (or disabled veterans, black Americans). We'd like to count you in for a recruitment ad for our publication.'' Or the caller may say something like, ''You advertised in our publication last year, and I know you'll want to run the advertisement again this year.'' In many cases, the caller is a fraud; there is no publication. Always ask to see a copy of the publication, and ask to see the ad your organization ran last year if that is the claim. Be wary of these unscrupulous organizations out to take advantage of your interest in recruiting these labor-market segments, but recognize that there are legitimate organizations as well that may make similar calls to your organization. Carefully check references to distinguish between these types of calls.

IDEA NO. 13: RECRUITING BLACKS, HISPANICS, ASIANS, INDIANS, AND OTHER MINORITY GROUPS

Recruitment Issues

One of the biggest myths about recruiting minority groups is that a single message or activity, targeted to a single minority group, will be effective in attracting all minorities. In fact, to be effective, recruitment must be extremely targeted, even within the minority group.

For example, there has been a notion that to attract Hispanics an employer merely needed to advertise in Spanish. One employer discovered that when they used a ''generic'' Spanish voice with Mexican music, their message appealed to Mexicans, but not to Puerto Ricans, Cubans, and other Hispanic groups. A generic approach, even within this subset of Hispanic targeting, was ineffective in achieving its goals.[5]

If there seems to be a common goal or need among minority applicants, it is in the search for an employer that will recognize the importance of offering opportunities for growth and advancement, and a work environment not just free of discrimination, but one that celebrates diversity. Minority candidates want to work in an atmosphere of acceptance and equity.

Corning Glass Works recognized that if they were to continue to recruit minorities and women, they needed to do a better job in retaining these employees. According to *The Wall Street Journal*, between 1980 and 1987 1 in 14 male professionals left Corning, while 1 in 6 black professionals left, as did 1 in 7 female professionals. In an exit interview, females and minorities cited ''lack of career opportunities'' as the reason for leaving.

When Corning conducted a formal study, it discovered that many of the informal communications lines and avenues for advancement were closed to minorities and females. For example, they were excluded from informal get-togethers or ignored at meetings. Other obstacles facing minorities, according to Harbridge House Inc., may include absence of performance feedback, lack of mentoring, little formal career guidance, and erroneous assumptions about assignments they will accept.

Corning also faced another problem in its remote location in rural, up-state New York. Blacks and females were not interested in small-town life for fear of isolation. Many blacks, for example, were having to drive an hour or more to Ithaca or Rochester for a haircut, since there were no black hairdressers in town. Corning decided to attract a black hairdresser and is working to draw other minority businesses to the area.

Corning also offered diversity training to its managers and has made commitment to affirmative action a goal for all management.

Interviewing skills must also take into consideration the diversity issues, according to Jim Kennedy, president of Management Team Consultants, Inc. in San Francisco. Interviewers with traditional American values may have expectations of eye contact, facial expressiveness, and a selling approach from the candidate. However, with different cultural backgrounds, these expectations may not be met. Recruiters must be aware of the role diversity plays throughout the staffing process.[6]

Certainly, in recruiting minorities and candidates of ethnic diversity, an organization must consider a total approach to staffing in order not just to recruit but to retain this labor-market segment.

Targeted Recruitment Activities

There are a number of organizations that can assist you in your search for qualified minority candidates. The National Urban League is one of the largest minority organizations with employment programs that can help you in targeting minorities. Your local Private Industry Council (PIC) can also provide some information about resources in your community committed to employment assistance to a variety of minority groups.

In addition to these organizations, here are some additional recruitment activities that can be targeted to attract minorities:

- Employee referral—to the extent that your organization already employs minorities, capitalize on this resource and work with minority employees to gain referrals, as well as information, on making your organization a better place for minorities.

- Ethnic and minority newspapers—there are a number of newspapers targeted to black, Japanese, Chinese, Filipino, Korean, Malayan, Vietnamese, and Hispanic readers, particularly in the larger metropolitan areas. Contact your recruitment-advertising agency for a listing of such publications in your area.

- Minority colleges and universities—recruit here to attract top-notch minority graduates (see Chapter Six on college recruiting).

- Career and job fairs targeted for minority candidates—participate in these fairs, often sponsored by colleges and other organizations.

- Posters and pictures of minority candidates in recruitment literature.

- Direct mail—send messages that appeal to minority candidates by purchasing a mailing list of these candidates.

- Magazines and trade journals—advertise in these publications targeted to minorities.

Another recruitment activity to attract minorities includes the use of minority graduate databases, such as those available through McClure-Lundbert Associates, Inc., a firm that sells this information to employers. The database is a PC-compatible product, or can be purchased in hardcopy format. McClure-Lundbert makes available mailing labels, yearly subscriptions to selective databases or the full database, as well as directories of minority college graduates.

HispanData is a national Hispanic résumé database, owned by Hispanic Business, Inc. in Santa Barbara, California. Companies can opt for a corporate membership with unlimited access, or can pay an individual membership fee to list up to 10 positions. Candidates pay a nominal fee to be included in the database.[7]

Many organizations are developing a multimedia approach to minority recruitment, as did one police force in a recent media campaign. Because of a recent consent decree, a large majority of their hires were to be blacks, Hispanics, and women. There were also informal goals to attract Asians.

Specific problems included a negative public image, as well as a limited budget of $30,000. The police force developed a commercial within the budget constrictions, with 10-, 15-, and 30-second spots, both in English and Spanish versions. A picture of a black male officer is shown, fading to a picture of an Hispanic female officer, fading to an Asian male officer, and so on. All the people shown were actual police officers. The narrator says, "Our cops only come in one color. Blue. Be somebody. Be a cop." The telephone number displays at the end of the ad.

The ad was used as a public service announcement (PSA), and was the most popular PSA in terms of airtime after the commercial, "This is your brain; this is your brain on drugs."

In addition to the targeted advertisement, the organization also took a look at the application process and made some changes that made it easier for candidates to apply.[8]

Targeted Recruitment Messages

While generic approaches will attract some minorities, the more focused recruitment approach is more effective. Consider the following:

- "Advancement opportunities"—minority candidates want to know that they have the chance at the entry-level job, and at continuing management opportunities on up the ladder.
- "Extensive training offered"—candidates want to see that the tools are available for their continued success on the job.
- "Equal Opportunity Employer"—minority candidates want proof that the organization is committed to affirmative action.
- "We want people just like you"—candidates need to know, through pictures and other testimonial approaches, that minority candidates are actively sought after by the organization.

A picture of Cindy Richmond is featured in a McDonnell Douglas one-page recruitment advertisement. She states in this testimonial approach, "Education is sort of a pet project of mine here in our department. I push it as hard as I can. So, a while back, I got our group together to talk about it—how going back to school could make our department and our job a better place, maybe give some people a new outlook, open all of us up to new ideas. We had some people from the University come in to brief us on programs available. That really got things rolling. The first group of us graduated just last spring. The results are fantastic. I've seen people who were kind of dead set in their ways become more open, relaxed, confident. And have more new options opened to them. For me in my career, education is everything."

Another full-page, four-color recruitment advertisement features a picture of a minority, with the heading, "They say a liberal arts degree will get you nowhere. Look where it got me." This Prudential advertisement goes on to entice liberal arts graduates to consider the career options with their company.

Be aware of the subtle messages that you send to candidates during the application and interview process. Do you have minority magazines in your reception area where candidates wait for their next interview? Do minority candidates see other minorities working in the organization? Are there minorities throughout the organization, not just in entry-level jobs? Are minority candidates scheduled to talk with other minority professionals? Ask these questions to ensure you are sending the right message to minority applicants.

IDEA NO. 14: IMMIGRANTS

Recruitment Issues

Immigrants are faced with a variety of challenges in adjusting to their new home—family members left behind, a new and confusing language, a new culture with new values and ethics, and uncertain support system.

Often, what immigrants need are the opportunities for basic skills training, including English classes, networking to establish new friends and a new support system, information on resources available in the community, and a chance to prove capabilities in order to advance within an organization.

This is what Victor Vongs, general manager of the Holiday Inn Crowne Plaza in White Plains, New York, discovered in building a strong human resources program. When Vongs was assigned the property, the hotel was facing low employee morale, high turnover, and an unprofitable outlook. With a high percentage (85 percent) of immigrants as employees, Vongs, a Thai native, took action on these issues.

Finding a first home is difficult for many of these employees, so Vongs takes an active role with his real estate contacts, providing a listing of available housing to his employees. Vongs also arranges English classes, held at a local high school. Informal meetings with employees, with bilingual employees serving as translators, help during the transitional period.

Employees at the Holiday Inn Crowne also have the opportunities to be rewarded for exceptional performance, with a number of ways to be recognized. Career paths for all positions are part of the plan to keep employees motivated beyond the entry-level, low-paying jobs.

The dividends have paid off. Vongs has reduced turnover from 83 percent to 11 percent, and has increased net revenues from $328,000 in 1987 to $2 million in 1989. Vongs attributes his attention to the unique needs of this employee group in permitting him to achieve his business goals.[9]

Employers should also be aware of the changing laws and regulations regarding the employment of immigrants. Contact the regional immigration office for detailed information regarding employers' obligations.

Targeted Recruitment Activities

Employers can attract immigrants to the workplace in a number of ways. Consider the following ideas:

- Develop messages for radio stations with listener demographics that meet your target audience.
- Advertise in ethnic and community newspapers with a targeted message.
- Use employee referral to recruit more immigrants.
- Work with government-funded programs and other community-based programs offering assistance to immigrants, such as the Soviet Employment Program, a division of the Philadelphia-based Jewish Employment and Vocational Service, providing employment services to Soviet immigrants.
- Post notices at community colleges and other locations that sponsor English-as-a-second-language classes.
- Sponsor your own English class for employees, and if possible, extend the class to nonemployees, using this as a means to recruit more employees!

Targeted Recruitment Messages

Recruitment messages, like all of the targeted messages for other labor-market segments, should let the audience know that they are wanted. Identify with their needs for basic skills training, English classes, networking, and advancement opportunities, and make these a strong part of the ad.

Offer versions of the ad in English and in the first language of the population you seek to employ.

IDEA NO. 15: RECRUITING WOMEN

Recruitment Issues

While some may believe that women leave their place of employment to address home and family issues, recent studies have shown otherwise. One study, called "Don't Blame the Baby," conducted by Wick and Co., a Wilmington, Delaware-based firm, found that the number one reason for women leaving their job was the perception of being blocked from career growth. The study found that women are less tolerant than men in staying in jobs that are dissatisfying. Of those women leaving their jobs, 73 percent went to work for other employers, 13 percent started their own businesses, and 7 percent were in between jobs. Most notable was that 77 percent of the men surveyed indicated they would likely stay with their company if dissatisfied, versus only 35 percent of the women.

Victoria Tashjian, vice president of Wick and Co., states, "Women seem to feel more comfortable making a change. They feel that they have paid a high price for having a career, and they want payback."[10]

Child care (and increasingly, elder care) is still an important element for any organization focusing on attracting employees today, particularly those women who still maintain the traditional role of providing care for family members.

Increasingly, organizations are offering child care options as a means to recruit and retain employees. America West Airlines, headquartered in Phoenix, Arizona, is one such company. It provides 24-hour, seven-days-a-week care services, with options for a home-based care program or a center-based plan. As stated by Michael Conway, president of the company, "It's a critical need that companies that can afford it will meet because it's the right thing to do. Even companies that have limited means may be forced to support child care from a competitive standpoint, to attract, retain, and motivate personnel."[11]

Like many other labor-market segments, this population is quite diverse in terms of needs, motivations, and issues of employment. There are those women entering the workplace for the first time—"first-timers"; those who are reentrants—"returners"; those women who want to change their career direction—"career shifters"; and those who want to advance within their chosen career field—"advancers." Each of these subsets will have different employment needs, and will respond to different types of recruitment activities and messages.

First-timers, those new to the world of work with their first "real" job out of school, are looking for a chance to prove themselves. Use school recruitment activities to attract women with the kind of skills training and education necessary to do the job.

Returners, those who are reentering the job market, often after an absence due to time spent raising a family, will be most interested in ways to update their skills and abilities, and become acclimated to the new work environment quickly. Returners will be looking for reentrant skills training, special classes to fine-tune and update their knowledge. Hospitals are finding these programs useful in attracting back to the workplace those nurses who have left the field and are now interested in returning.

Returners may also be reluctant to return, unsure of their skills and abilities. Activities that gently sell the benefits of employment are particularly appealing to this group, in the form of career fairs and information seminars. Rich's Department Stores and TempWorld in Atlanta have discovered the information seminar to be an excellent method for attracting returners.

Some returners may be "reluctant returners"—often called displaced homemakers. These are women who are now forced into the workplace due to the death of a spouse, divorce, or an abusive home situation. Employers seeking to reach this group can find assistance with the Displaced Homemaker Network, with local programs operating across the United States (see the Appendix for further information).

Career shifters are those women who might consider a career change from one industry or occupation to another. Retailers and other service industry companies are looking to other industries and occupations where they have a selling advantage—an opportunity to attract women into new careers paying higher wages, offering better benefits or working conditions or more flexible schedules. Again, open houses, career and job fairs, and information seminars are excellent activities to discuss these possibilities with women in other careers. Some employers may be seeking women as "career shifters" to fill nontraditional roles. Similar activities are successful in making these opportunities known to women.

Advancers can be attracted by more traditional forms of recruitment, because the recruiter can usually identify where these women are already working. Telemarketing (or telerecruiting) might be one way to reach these women. Direct mail, agencies, and other more intrusive forms of recruitment may be best, as many of these women are already happily employed someplace else.

Targeted Recruitment Activities

Women can respond to a number of targeted recruitment activities, including the following:

- Open houses targeted to women, offering free child care during the event.

- Information seminars focusing on job-search skills, update on specific job skills, dressing for the job, and child care options, as well as information seminars on state-of-the-art technology for women in professional and technical occupations.

- Career and job fairs sponsored by women's organizations.

- Networking with professional and business organizations for women, such as the local chapter of the Business and Professional Women. Offer to give a talk, sponsor an event, and get to know the members. Many chapters may even have a formal placement service.

- Join forces with government-funded programs and other organizations offering employment services to women. Contact the local Private Industry Council or the local YWCA for names of these organizations.

- Develop targeted recruitment advertisements, and place them in newspaper sections with high readership of women—living sections, food sections, and business sections. One employer placed an ad in the grocery store coupon ad section, with the ad resembling a clip-out coupon for effect.

- Place targeted posters in places frequented by women going about their daily activities—grocery stores, banks, laundromats, pharmacies, libraries, schools.

- Use telemarketing to reach women. One Hallmark card-shop manager found great success in calling the other mothers whose names appeared in her child's nursery school directory. She introduced herself as ''Joey's mother,'' and also as the local Hallmark manager, and asked these moms if they knew of anyone who might like to work at the local card shop part-time. This low-cost strategy was a huge success in filling some hard-to-recruit part-time positions.

Targeted Recruitment Messages

Appeal to women readers by demonstrating your organization's commitment to training, advancement opportunities, and flexibility. If you offer some sort of child care program, sell this benefit in the advertisement. Attract women by identifying with their desire for team spirit and cooperation, and the chance to build self-confidence and self-esteem.

Use pictures of women, including testimonials, to further target recruitment messages. Check all recruitment literature and advertisements to ensure representation.

Red Lobster uses an appealing headline, along with ad copy that appeals to many potential women candidates. The headlines read, "Every day is Mother's Day at Red Lobster," with bulleted features of employment listed:

- Full-/part-time hours.
- Flexible scheduling.
- Great starting salary.
- Profit sharing/savings plan.
- Paid vacations/holidays.
- Eligibility for group health/dental insurance.
- Meal discounts.
- Training and advancement.

Dean Witter uses a targeted approach in both the medium and the message. It has developed a series of full-page advertisements appearing in *Working Woman* magazine. The 1990 ad campaign featured different women, providing a testimonial-type approach. One ad began with the headline, "A most valuable asset," with a large black and white photograph of Karen Gibbs, a black female executive with Dean Witter. Karen says in the ad, "Here at Dean Witter, I have the benefit of working with a top-rated research department and first-rate co-workers." The ad goes on to say that the company is looking for more people like Karen Gibbs, with information about how to contact the company.

A second ad features Kathy Tully, a vice president and assistant branch manager with the company. Tully states, "I'm no wonder woman. Dean

Witter works as hard for me as I do for Dean Witter. They give you the training, the products, and incentive programs. I just took advantage of them.''

The 1991 ad features a similar approach, this time with the headline, ''We're looking for people who chart their own course. Like Elizabeth Jones.'' Jones is featured with a brief statement explaining her role in piloting a financial-planning seminar on a cruise ship one week each year. Jones says in the ad, ''You're always moving moving moving. As a broker, I'm always on top of something new, exploring what's best for each of my clients. It starts with training. Intense. The best. For advanced training, they sent me to San Francisco for a month. Dean Witter makes sure you're prepared.''

IDEA NO. 16: ATTRACTING TEENS AND INFLUENCING "INFLUENCERS"

Recruitment Issues

Increasingly, employers are looking to teen workers as a means not just to meet staffing needs, but as a method to develop alliances with these workers, hoping to recruit and retain them later for other positions. With the baby bust a reality, organizations are having to work even harder to attract their fair share of the best young workers available.

Hardee's Food Systems, a traditional recruiter of teen workers, understands that they must work harder to attract the same quality, and quantity, of young workers they have employed in the past. Therefore, in addition to targeted recruitment and retention programs on employment initiatives for older workers (''New Horizons'') and persons with disabilities (''Capabilities''), Hardee's introduced their ''FastTracks'' program.

FastTracks provided training for restaurant managers on new ideas for recruiting and retaining teens. It began with focus groups with young workers across the country to learn about the issues and opportunities in employing youth.

Hardee's teens were very sensitive to their work uniform, and wanted, at the very least, clean uniforms that fitted properly. They also had a real need for flexibility in work schedules, since most of them were balancing school activities, studies, friends, boyfriends and girlfriends, and home responsibilities. Many young workers were working to put themselves through college or vocational school, so scholarships were appealing. Finally, and perhaps most importantly, they craved being treated as adults. Many of the teens in focus groups complained that they were often treated as second-class citizens, and wanted the chance to be thought of by their managers as an important asset to the restaurant.

In this program, Hardee's also learned about important corecruiters—teachers, counselors, and parents. These "influencers" often participated in making the employment decision, and wanted more information about employment for their students/children. As a result, Hardee's developed two lines of recruitment materials, one set aimed at the teen, and another set of materials focused on the concerns of parents and teachers, the influencers.

Be aware of local child labor laws that will impact how you manage workers under 18 years of age. Usually there are much stricter guidelines for workers 14 and 15 years of age and for workers ages 16 to 17. Contact your wage and hour representative from the Department of Labor for information on restrictions for hours and work duties in your state.

Targeted Recruitment Activities

Since there are virtually two markets in recruiting teens—the primary market of teens, and the secondary market including teen influencers, recruitment activities for each will be outlined separately.

Influencer recruitment activities can include:

- Advertise in major metropolitan papers and community newspapers talking about jobs for sons and daughters.
- Develop recruitment brochures and literature targeted to parents and teachers. Hardee's developed an influencer piece, which contained complete sentences (the teen brochure had bulleted points to give it a "hip" quality) and less "hype" and teen jargon, appealing to this group.
- Consider business-education partnerships that are being developed across the country, many in conjunction with the National Alliance for Business, chambers of commerce, boards of education, and business leaders.
- Participate in an "adopt-a-school" program.
- Provide a presentation to a class on careers in your industry, or on job search skills.

- Develop surveys to be sent to high school teachers, counselors, and parents about what they want in a high school student's work experience.
- Create a newsletter for teens, as well as for their parents and teachers.
- Participate in high school career fairs.
- Sponsor high school team and club events.

Teen recruitment activities can include:

- Advertise in high school newspapers, yearbooks, and rosters.
- Place posters on high school bulletin boards.
- Develop a task force of high school students. Some employers develop a teen board to promote student involvement.
- Work with a Junior Achievement class.
- Hold an open house targeted to students.
- Send direct-mail letters to teens.
- Work with vocational education programs, such as the Distributive Education Clubs of America (DECA).
- Offer a scholarship program as a means to recruit and retain workers.
- Hold an awards banquet for young workers, with recognition given to those who most successfully balance school and work.

Targeted Recruitment Messages

The army has recognized the importance of influencers in recruitment and has developed targeted messages to appeal to this segment. A full-page, four-color advertisement appearing in *Time* magazine shows a picture of a woman hugging a young man in uniform. The headlines read, ''Letting my son join the army was the hardest thing I've ever done. It was also one of the smartest.'' The ad copy goes on to read, ''Russ has always been the baby of our family, so I was terribly upset the day he left us for the army. Even though I knew he had good reasons for joining—especially the money he'd be earning for college—I also knew how tough the army could be. And I worried about how he would cope. Then, three months later, I was invited to Russell's graduation from basic training. As I watched him standing there—looking so strong, so mature, so self-confident—I realized the army had done something really important for my son. It had helped him grow up. And believe me, if you think Russell felt proud that day, you should have seen his mother." The ad copy concluded with a toll-free number to call for more information for the readers' son or daughter.

Messages for teens should include benefits they will experience on the job, which may include flexibility in work schedules, a fun work environment, money for the extras, learning about the world of work skills, respect, friends, and money and benefits to support their families.

IDEA NO. 17: APPEALING TO THE "TWENTYSOMETHING" GENERATION

Recruitment Issues

Attracting the "twentysomething" generation, those graduating from school to enter the world of work for the first time, can be a challenge, and even a headache for some recruiters. Also called "baby busters" or the "birth dearth" generation, there are fewer of these workers to attract, especially when compared to the baby boomer generation (baby boomers represented almost 72.5 million births; baby busters represented only about 56.6 million births). Further, the values and work ethic of these workers are significantly different than their older counterparts. As stated in an article appearing in *Working Woman* magazine (August 1990), these employees "have an attitude. They want access, authority, and answers—and they want it all *now.*" Another article in *Time* magazine (July 16, 1990) concludes that this generation "is balking at work, marriage, and baby boomer values."

What do these workers want? They do have a different set of values, which includes the need for independence, for work- and home-life balance, and for quality and not status. They value education and want alternatives in their lives. They are loyal to themselves and are motivated to find happiness and personal satisfaction more so than their older counterparts. One bumper sticker, with a twentysomething driver, proudly displayed this message, "Hard work never hurt anyone . . . but why take chances." Another baby buster coffee mug displayed the message, "Party forever, work whenever."

It used to be that young workers, or "first careerists," tended to stay with an organization until something caused them to leave. Contemporary first careerists, however, "tend to leave unless some force encourages them to stay," state authors Marcia A. Manter and Janice Y. Benjamin in "How to Hold on to First Careerists" (*Personnel Administrator,* September 1989).

In a recent survey conducted by the Society for Human Resource Management, reported in *HRNews*, human resources professionals stated that the most popular programs to entice first careerists included increase employee participation in decision making, increase training opportunities, review/emphasize employee orientation, emphasize/improve benefits, and add job variety/important tasks.[12]

Targeted Recruitment Activities

Targeted recruitment activities are usually those focused on students—college, vocational, or high school—who are looking for their first job. Use these traditional methods to attract twentysomething generation candidates (review Chapter Six on school recruiting strategies).

Targeted Recruitment Messages

Messages for this group should appeal to their values and interests. Consider the message used in one classified ad, obviously attempting to attract twentysomething generation candidates:

> No experience please. International wholesale company has various positions available. Wild and crazy office. Fun, relaxed atmosphere. Serious pay, ($300–$500+ weekly salary potential) while working with nonserious people. First come, first served. Call xxx-xxxx.

For specific messages to use in recruitment, consider demonstrating the advantages of employment that appeal most to this generation. Stress their involvement in the work environment, training and cross-training opportunities, work alternatives and options, job variety, and personal satisfaction. Then, develop strong new-employee orientation programs to bond these new employees to the organization in an attempt to retain these elusive candidates.

IDEA NO. 18: ATTRACTING EXITING AND RETIRING MILITARY

Recruitment Issues

Exiting and retiring military personnel can be another source of qualified candidates to consider for open positions. Many of these candidates have a steady employment record, years of experience, and skills and training necessary to perform a number of civilian occupations.

Often, one of the biggest hurdles for exiting and retiring military in finding employment is in translating their military experience into civilian terms and jargon. Any human resource manager who has seen military résumés will affirm that they are usually 10 pages long and contain terms and jargon that only a 10-year military veteran could understand!

Many employers are providing assistance to exiting military by offering specialized services, either on military bases or in an open-house format, on job-search strategies, including information on preparing a résumé. They are using this opportunity to talk about career options within their organizations, and finding good employees as the outcome.

Targeted Recruitment Activities

The army is making it easy for interested employers to work with them, and has developed a booklet, *Experience for Hire,* which documents the qualifications of army "alumni" and explains how these individuals can meet staffing goals for civilian employers. The booklet also discusses a new program designed to work directly with employers, called Army Career and Alumni Program (ACAP). The booklet states that the army will ultimately have over 50 job-assistance centers worldwide. See the Appendix for contact information.

Other recruitment activities can include the following:

- Targeted recruitment ads in military newspapers and publications.
- Participation in job fairs, sponsored by the military for its exiting personnel.
- Checking the yellow pages under "U.S. Government" for the number of the nearest military unit to determine the types of specialties serving reservists might offer.
- Sponsoring an information seminar for military personnel by working with the military base in your area.

Targeted Recruitment Messages

Targeted recruitment messages for exiting and retiring military should communicate the opportunity to put their years of experience and training within the military to use in a civilian occupation.

IDEA NO. 19: ATTRACTING CAREER SHIFTERS

Recruitment Issues, Activities, and Messages

Career shifters are those individuals who are considering a change in their career direction. They are an important market target, particularly if your industry is facing a labor shortage and must begin to attract more individuals to consider employment in your field.

People who are considering such a change will need information and time to weigh the options. Therefore, a recruitment approach should not attempt to "close the sale" quickly, but rather, permit candidates the chance to gain a lot of information before making up their minds.

Open houses are an excellent activity for career shifters, as they do not involve an immediate, structured interview process, but instead, an informal chance for the candidate to gain information and discuss concerns and issues. Many employers are developing open houses specifically for career shifters, and advertise for the event with the message, "Are you considering a career move . . . come to our open house and check us out."

Another strategy to use in attracting career shifters is to consider what labor-market segment may be most attracted by the opportunities that you have. For example, a bank with low-wage teller positions offering a beautiful work environment may target low-wage earners in a manufacturing setting. Or an insurance company offering highly competitive salary and benefits packages may target low-wage earners.

IDEA NO. 20: WORKING WITH MOONLIGHTERS

Recruitment Issues, Activities, and Messages

Increasingly, moonlighters—those who work two or more jobs—are working not just for the money, but also to explore other career options. Therefore, this market segment can be very attractive, since they are potential career shifters. Employers are beginning to entice these workers, instead of discouraging them, to explore the job opportunities within their industry.

Moonlighters' greatest employment need is flexibility. They need to be able to juggle their job schedules, along with home and family commitments. Many of these individuals are interested in part-time work schedules, as well as nonpeak hours. Advertise flexibility as one of your benefits if you can offer it.

Appeal to moonlighters directly through targeted testimonial type ads. Consider addressing your advertisement directly to people who may be interested in a second job: students, police officers and firefighters (who have irregular schedules), health care workers, teachers.

IDEA NO. 21: WORKING WITH PRISON-RELEASE PROGRAMS

Recruitment Issues, Activities, and Messages

Another source of nontraditional employees is through prison-release programs. Contact the personnel officer or counselor at the prison to discuss your employment needs, and work closely with these individuals to ensure a successful program.

Consider the sensitivity of the position, reaction from customers and co-workers, and other issues before beginning such an endeavor. Consult with top management and with legal counsel to ensure total organizational commitment to this program before beginning.

IDEA NO. 22: HIRING THE HOMELESS

Recruitment Issues, Activities, and Messages

Days Inn, based in Atlanta, Georgia, has developed a model program for employing the homeless in their budget motel chain across the country. Other organizations are following the example, and have targeted this population as a means not just to reach staffing goals, but to give something back to the community.

In working with the homeless, contact local public agencies that provide services to these groups. Establish resources available to this employee group, and guidelines for implementation before initiating.

IDEA NO. 23: TURNING CUSTOMERS INTO EMPLOYEES

Recruitment Issues, Activities, and Messages

Are your customers a good potential labor-market segment for you to consider? If so, think about ways you can reach out to this group. One department store with their own charge customers included a flyer with their monthly bill, saying, ''Your bill could be reduced by 10 percent if you were an employee!''

One Hallmark manager was paying attention to an older customer who came into the store to purchase several gifts. The manager asked whom the gifts were for, and the customer shared, with some sadness, that she was retiring from her job, and had bought some gifts for her co-workers. The manager asked her if she would consider working part-time at Hallmark, and the customer said, ''Yes!''

Retailers aren't the only ones who can use this approach, although they perhaps have the easiest opportunity to target customers. One hospital placed a recruitment poster in the cafeteria and found some success. For more ideas on point of sale recruitment, refer to Chapter Three.

IDEA NO. 24: HIRING BACK FORMER EMPLOYEES AND RETIREES

Recruitment Issues, Activities, and Messages

Sometimes your best former employees can make your best future employees, if you develop specific strategies to identify and target this market. One employer who had recently lost several employees to a new competitor called these employees back after 90 days to conduct an exit interview. During the interview, the company representative asked how things were going with their new employer and discovered that the new employees were not happy. The representative extended job offers and the former employees returned, remaining loyal to their first employer since learning the grass wasn't necessarily greener on the other side!

One employer decided to use this strategy and called all employees who had left that year. One problem occurred: the caller did not carefully

screen who was being called, and a former employee who had been terminated for cause was accidentally invited back.

Retirees are another former employee group that might be targeted for
recruitment. The Travelers successfully attracts their retired employees
for temporary "pool" positions through "unretirement" parties. Refer to
the section in this chapter on older workers for additional information.

It's been said, "If you always do what you always did, you'll always get
what you always got!" So true in recruitment today. Employers must begin to try new, targeted strategies in order to attract those employee groups
needed for employment. In fact, one recruiter recently said, "If you always do what you always did, you won't even get what you used to get,"
which is even more true today!

Ideas for Recruiting the Workforce 2000

Idea No. 11: Recruiting older workers.

Idea No. 12: Attracting persons with disabilities.

Idea No. 13: Recruiting blacks, Hispanics, Asians, Indians, and other minority groups.

Idea No. 14: Recruiting immigrants.

Idea No. 15: Recruiting women.

Idea No. 16: Attracting teens and influencing "influencers."

Idea No. 17: Appealing to the "twentysomething" generation.

Idea No. 18: Attracting exiting and retiring military.

Idea No. 19: Attracting career shifters.

Idea No. 20: Working with moonlighters.

Idea No. 21: Working with prison-release programs.

Idea No. 22: Hiring the homeless.

Idea No. 23: Turning customers into employees.

Idea No. 24: Hiring back former employees and retirees.

Ideas for Recruiting the Workforce 2000

Idea	Cost	Number People	Lead Time	Target
Idea No. 11: Older workers	L–H	—	S–L	—
Idea No. 12: People with disabilities	L–H	—	S–L	—
Idea No. 13: Minority groups	L–H	—	S–L	—
Idea No. 14: Immigrants	L–H	—	S–L	—
Idea No. 15: Women	L–H	—	S–L	—
Idea No. 16: Teens	L–H	—	S–L	—
Idea No. 17: "Twentysomething-ers"	L–H	—	S–L	—
Idea No. 18: Retiring military	L–H	—	S–L	—
Idea No. 19: Career shifters	L–H	—	S–L	—
Idea No. 20: Moonlighters	L–H	—	S–L	—
Idea No. 21: Prison-release programs	L	—	S–L	—
Idea No. 22: The homeless	L	—	S–L	—
Idea No. 23: Customers	L–H	—	S–L	—
Idea No. 24: Former employees	L–H	—	S–L	—

Key:

Cost		Lead time	
Low	0–$200	Short	0–1 week
Medium	$200–$1,000	Moderate	1 week–4 weeks
High	$1,000+	Long	4+ weeks
Number people		Target	
Single	1	Yes	
Multiple	2 or more	No	
Either			

ENDNOTES

1. Catherine D. Fyock, *America's Work Force Is Coming of Age: What Every Business Needs to Know to Recruit, Train, Manage, and Retain an Aging Work Force* (Lexington, Mass.: Lexington Books, 1990), pp. 46–48.

2. Ibid., pp. 81–91.

3. Michelle Neely Martinez, "Creative Ways to Employ People with Disabilities," *HRMagazine,* November 1990, p. 101.

4. "Minority Brochure Features Braille," *Recruitment Today,* Fall 1990, p. 25.

5. Gladys M. Rosa, "Minority Recruiting," *Recruiting Magazine,* May/June 1990, p. 7.

6. William H. Wagel and Hermine Sagat Levine, "HR '90: Challenges and Opportunities," *Personnel,* June 1990, p. 19.

7. Jennifer J. Koch, "Finding Qualified Hispanic Candidates," *Recruitment Today,* Spring 1990, p. 35.

8. Tim Chauran, "Color Me Blue," *Recruitment Today,* February/March 1989, pp. 42–47.

9. Lorraine Calvert, "Helping Immigrants Adapt Stabilizes a Work Force," *Working Woman,* January 1990, p. 84.

10. Kathhryn Scovel, "Personnel Update," *Human Resource Executive,* June 1990, p. 22.

11. Elanna Yalow, "Corporate Child Care Helps Recruit and Retain Workers," *Personnel Journal,* June 1990, p. 48.

12. David Stier, "Good Policies Keep First Careerists," *HRNews,* April 1990, p. 2.

Chapter Three

Using Nontraditional
Recruiting Activities

W hen the going gets tough for recruiters, smart recruiters begin to think tough about creative ways to reach prospective job candidates. Thinking tough can include more intrusive ways to reach candidates when they aren't actively seeking employment, as in telemarketing, direct mail, and radio and television. And more than ever, it means trying new, nontraditional methods that haven't been fully exploited by those looking for the best candidates.

Some of the ideas presented in this chapter are a bit controversial, especially those that intrude upon the candidate at the work site. Some of these ethical issues are raised for your organization's consideration.

IDEA NO. 25: TELEMARKETING (TELERECRUITING)

What is telemarketing, when used in a recruitment setting? Telemarketing is the direct calling of prospective candidates, at home or on the job, to determine if there is interest in an employment opportunity.

Telemarketing is an activity that has traditionally been conducted by third-party recruiters—executive search firms and recruitment agencies. Increasingly, however, employers are reviewing the costs associated with these services, and making decisions to move this work in-house for a fraction of the cost.

What are the steps involved in planning a telemarketing plan? Consider these guidelines:

1. Discuss the plan of action with top management, especially if you are going to be contacting candidates at their current place of employment, and particularly if the candidates are working for a direct competitor or if

candidates have not expressed some prior interest in your organization. Many employers are not too pleased when they learn that a competitor is calling their employees at work, and several CEOs have been known to pick up the phone and call the CEO whose company is participating in telemarketing activities. In cases like this, your CEO should know what you are doing and should be in on the decision to ensure consistency with corporate philosophies. Also, consider whether or not your direct recruitment is really raiding, which may have legal consequences (refer to the next section in this chapter for further information).

2. The next step involves identifying the target market for your telemarketing efforts. Candidates may be identified by the job title they currently hold, by a professional or trade association of which they are a member, by certification or licensing held, or by virtue of graduation from a school or program. Candidates to be contacted may even be identified as past employees who left under favorable circumstances, or as participants in a past career fair or open house. Candidates to be contacted might also be those with active résumés or applications on file, or those who have been referred by current employees.

Do you want to reach these individuals at home or at work? Do you have their numbers? Which is more cost- and time-effective? If they are to be called at work, can you identify the desired candidates by title? If so, can you reach the candidate when there are staff who are screening callers? Answer these questions to determine which approach makes the most sense.

3. Next in the process is determining how phone numbers are to be elicited. You can develop calling lists by identifying company names with likely candidates (look up numbers in the phone book), by reviewing application/résumé files and records from past career fairs and open houses, or through a roster or membership directory (of a club, organization, school, or place of worship). Telephone numbers, like mailing lists, can also be purchased from companies specializing in these data services (see direct mail for further information). There are also companies that develop candidate databases, charging a fee to candidates who wish to be listed. Many of these are specialized by occupation or by labor-market group (Hispanic, blacks, older workers, etc.).

4. Once the telephone numbers have been identified, the next step is deciding who will be conducting the calls and what the posturing will be. For example, will you be hiring a third party to make calls for you, or will you make the calls in-house? Employers can work with a recruitment agency or can hire an independent contractor, such as a consultant, to con-

duct the calls for you. If you decide to make the calls in-house, will the callers identify themselves to the candidates as company representatives? At what point? One employer chose to use in-house staff, but decided that the company would not reveal its identity until the candidate had indicated some initial interest.

Recognize that whoever you select to do the calling should have some sales skills and should be comfortable talking with people on the telephone. Involve your sales department, if you have one, to gain some ideas for instructing your caller.

5. Developing the script is the next step in the process. What questions do you want to ask candidates? Many employers have found that one of the best side benefits of telemarketing—other than recruiting candidates—is in gaining information about what the competitive labor issues are. For example, one employer learned that they offered the best training program in the industry and were perceived by candidates as having excellent opportunities for growth. Similarly, they learned that one competitor offered extraordinary pay to their management employees, making this competitor almost impenetrable for recruitment purposes.

Also, remember that you will be calling on candidates who may not even be at the "just shopping" stage, so your call will need to really sell the candidate on the reasons employment with your organization is something to consider. Plan questions to elicit what the candidate is interested in, and prepare benefits to present to the candidate.

Arrange in advance for the caller to have interview schedules available so that prospective candidates can immediately follow through on the interest generated by your call. Remember that they are already working, so make evening and weekend interview times available for their convenience.

6. Develop a form for callers to use in collecting data on candidates who are contacted. Analyze what information is most important for you to identify, such as job title and responsibilities—by company and by individual, current salary ranges, area of greatest job dissatisfaction, and job feature most desired in the next career move. Use this information to analyze your greatest recruitment strengths and weaknesses, and use this information to develop future recruitment strategies.

Also, maintain good records of who is contacted so that candidates are not contacted a second time. You don't want to appear desperate!

7. Set up interviews quickly; you are capitalizing on an "impulse buy" that should be followed up with more information to cement that initial

image. Remember that the initial interview should be a selling interview as much as a selection interview; you should be sure to sell the candidate on the job opportunities as much as you make a determination of job match. Train the interviewers on both selling and selection skills.

8. Make the hire decision as quickly as possible. Keep the candidate informed throughout the process, and follow up to maintain the candidate's interest. Try to establish deadlines for making employment decisions and stick to them.[1]

Apple Computer Inc. in Cupertino, California, uses telemarketing in a unique way to help meet their staffing needs. They joined forces with Telemarketing Solutions of Menlo Park to create a telerecruiting department of five staff members.

Apple uses the department to interview candidates who have responded over the phone to advertised positions and to create applicant résumés via the computer. This process speeds up the applicant process. Where it used to take the company 60 to 90 days to interview and hire candidates who had responded to ads, the company can now interview candidates in three days and make the selection decision in under three weeks.

Apple is convinced that the process has permitted them to hire better candidates, since many of the candidates today are "hidden." Gail Sheridan of Telemarketing Solutions says that these candidates are "already employed but are scanning what's available. For them, being able to respond easily and quickly is what may get them to raise their hands as interested applicants."[2]

The Pros and Cons of Telemarketing

Many companies are reluctant to use telemarketing, especially when it involves direct contact to candidates who have not previously expressed some interest in the organization. Some feel that contacting candidates at their place of business is unethical. Others feel that they need to rely on and work with their competitors in more collaborative ways (especially those employers in small communities), and see telemarketing as a conflict of this philosophy. Some feel that candidates who are not used to receiving these calls may see them as unprofessional and as a desperate move by the employer calling.

Other employers feel that, in a tight labor market, all's fair, including telemarketing campaigns. These employers also feel that direct calling to candidates is legitimate, especially since they have been paying third-party recruiters, such as recruitment agencies and executive-search firms, to perform this service for years. In fact, some employers argue that they prefer the idea of performing this service in-house, in that they can control how the calls are made, what is said, and can ensure that the activity is performed in an ethical and professional manner.

The decision as to whether or not your organization chooses telemarketing is up to you and your top management. Consider the response by candidates, the practice within your industry, how third-party recruiters have been used in the past, as well as how the telemarketing campaign will be designed as important factors in deciding whether this strategy is to be used, and if so, how it is to be used to be consistent with organizational philosophy.

Telemarketing, especially when it contacts employees of direct competitors, is usually a short-term solution to the staffing dilemma. The long-term solution is to attract more interested employees into your industry occupations and to develop strategies to keep good employees within your organization.

IDEA NO. 26: DIRECT RECRUITMENT

Direct recruitment is the practice of approaching candidates openly and directly to discuss the opportunities with your organization, without any prior interest demonstrated on the part of the candidate. The industries having the most opportunity to participate in this practice are those whose employees have direct customer contact, such as retail, hospitality, and financial services. In these environments, recruiters posing as customers enter the place of business in order to talk with employees about their employment opportunities.

Hiring more than one employee from a competitor can be considered raiding, especially if the intent or result of your activity is damage to the raided employer. In this case, raiding may be illegal, with the raiding employer having liability for damages caused by their actions.[3]

Often, direct recruitment ends up being a game of musical chairs. Company One direct-recruits Person A from Company Two. Company Two recruits Candidate B from Company Three. Company Three hires Person A from Company One. And so the game goes, with none of the companies meeting their staffing goals and everyone becoming frustrated in this game of no winners.

In a seminar, one recruiter from a major New York City department store told of such a game being played vigorously with a competitor. Candidates were going back and forth, from one organization to another, until the recruiters finally became totally frustrated and decided to call a truce. They ended up with a "gentlemen's agreement" not to directly recruit any more candidates from one another, and only to hire candidates who came in and applied on their own. They solved many problems, as the revolving door was at least slowed.

Direct recruiting can be done in a professional manner. Sacino's Formalwear, based in St. Petersburg, Florida, uses a "talent scout card" to give to service workers who demonstrate exceptional performance in their jobs. All Sacino's managers are given these cards, which are a bit bigger in size than a traditional business card. When a manager sees anyone—a grocery store clerk, a waitress at a restaurant, a bell boy at a hotel, a department store sales associate—doing a great job, the manager presents this exceptional performer with a talent scout card, that reads:

> We believe enthusiasm, integrity, and exceptional customer service are vital to success. That's why SACINO'S continues to search for people who possess this combination of talents. We are looking for full-time and part-time employees who are looking for an exciting place to grow. SACINO'S acknowledges and rewards exceptional performance.

The card ends with contact information, including a toll-free number.

It never hurts to be on the look-out for great talent. One recruiter always makes it a point to look for talent when she dines in restaurants, and may casually ask waiters, waitresses, and other staff how they like their jobs. She might, if she feels the climate is right, ask them if they have ever considered employment in her organization. If they seem interested, she hands them her business card and asks them to call her. She makes it a point not to intrude into their business operation, and always handles the encounter in a professional manner. She has had great success with this system and has hired some excellent employees this way.

Another professional and technical recruiter looks for opportunities when attending trade and professional shows. He attends the trade shows and receptions and casually meets and talks with employees from other companies. He also asks them about their satisfaction with their current employer, and, if he feels there is some hesitation, looks for the chance to talk about his employer and provides his business card.

Again, as in the case with telemarketing, the decision as to how, when, and where direct recruiting is right for your organization depends upon you and your corporate philosophy.

What if you are the victim of a direct-recruiting raid—real recruitment pirating? Are there any steps you can take to stop this annoying, and sometimes business-threatening practice when it gets out of hand?

Many employers have used the approach of having the CEO of one organization make contact, by phone or by mail, with the CEO of the guilty party. Other employers have taken a similar approach, having legal counsel make contact instead. In cases where pirating or raiding activities do cause a real business hardship, legal counsel should be consulted as to whether a case for interference with business relationships can be made, in which case suit can be brought against the raiding employer.

One ingenious employer was being victimized by a particularly vicious raid by a competitor. This company decided to do a number of things to diminish the impact of these activities. The first was to call a meeting of all employees to discuss what was happening. Management told its employees that they really wanted their employees to stay with them, that they valued them, and that they would continue to work hard with them, through task forces and employee meetings, to meet their needs and concerns. Then they introduced a new plan: for every business card from a competitive recruiter that was turned in to management, the employee would receive a $25 "bounty." What a great strategy, because the employee now saw a competitor's business card, not as an opportunity for another job, but as an opportunity for $25! The program was a tremendous success, with further raiding attempts having minimal impact on the company.

IDEA NO. 27: USING TELEVISION—MAJOR NETWORK COMMERCIALS, CABLE ADVERTISING, AND PUBLIC SERVICE ANNOUNCEMENTS (PSAs)

Television is a targeted medium for recruitment advertising. Any station can provide employers with detailed information on viewer demographics by programming and time periods. In this way, you can develop a targeted message to reach the candidates desired for recruitment purposes. One employer wanting to target young candidates found that new cable stations, such as Music Television (MTV), were excellent for reaching the desired market segment.

There is no way around the fact that most television advertising is expensive, especially if you are thinking about prime-time commercials. First is the expense for production. A top-notch commercial must be produced professionally, and production costs run anywhere from about $10,000 at a minimum for a 30- to 60-second spot, to upwards of $100,000. Most recruitment commercials produced are in the $25,000 to $40,000 range. Refer to Chapter Six for additional information on production costs incurred by two companies using television as part of their recruitment strategies.

Arranging for airtime can be an added expense, varying widely from market to market. The local station, as well as your recruitment advertising agency, can provide you with specific information for airtime costs.

Some employers are spending a considerable part of their budgets for production costs, but keep airtime costs at a minimum through the use of public service announcements (PSAs). Refer to Chapter Two for a case study of one police force's use of PSAs in an effective recruitment campaign for minority officers.

Cable television can provide another low-cost alternative to television commercials. In most markets, there are "community bulletin board" channels, providing messages that run on an ongoing basis for a period of time. In most markets, this advertising is affordable, and can offer employers another means to reach out to prospective candidates.

Look for other recruitment opportunities on television, such as "*CareerLine,*" a half-hour program on the Financial News Network (FNN). The program featured a 20-minute segment on general career information, with the remainder of airtime devoted to a listing of specific job opportunities.

FNN appealed to those wanting to target professional candidates with college degrees, aged 25 to 40. Advertisers participated in a five-minute interview "spotlight," or in a 90-second spot. For a fee of $14,000, employers received two five-minute segments and production expenses, and four airings of an employment message. The 90-second spots ran $3,500 for two airings.[4]

For maximum results, combine the use of television with other forms of advertising. For example, use a television ad that refers candidates to your ad in the Sunday newspaper, which communicates the details for an open house (refer to Chapter Six for examples of this open-house media blitz).

Television can also be excellent for creating image advertising. Work with your marketing and public relations departments to develop a total-image program for recruitment purposes. These departments may also have advertising dollars you can use.

McDonald's has used this kind of image advertising to its advantage in the employment arena. It has developed several popular ads, most notably the commercial featuring the older man on his first day of work, and the young Down's Syndrome employee. Neither of these commercials' main message was for employment; however, the message sent about McDonald's commitment to older workers and people with disabilities is heard loud and clear.

IDEA NO. 28: ADVERTISING ON THE RADIO, AND COMBINING PRINT WITH RADIO

Radio is another medium that can be targeted to the candidates you want to reach, by identifying listener demographics by station and time of day. Call your local station for this information, or work with your recruitment advertising agency.

Another advantage of radio is that it is intrusive, in that it reaches listeners who are not actively seeking employment.

Radio production costs are much lower than those for television, and many employers produce their messages in-house, or inexpensively through a studio. Also, many stations will produce the radio spot for you; others may offer to talk about your company in a more informal, unstructured way. Be sure you have a good understanding of who will be doing these spots for you, and ensure that the individuals involved understand the purpose and theme of your message.

One radio station in Atlanta, Georgia, features a service to employers and job seekers. Radio "Power 99 FM"—WAPW 99.7—airs a daily JobLine, airing produced 60-second spots about job opportunities. Listeners can call in, punching in a code connecting them to the JobLine hot line. The recorded message provides additional information on the position, qualifications, and contact information.

JobLine programs are offered to employers at different price levels. Level A offers 10 60-second spots for Monday through Sunday, 5:00 A.M. to midnight, plus a 60-second spot on the telephone recording. Level B offers employers exclusive early-week advertising schedules, with 10 spots to run morning and afternoon drive times, plus the recorded message. Level C provides employers with an exclusive advertising schedule, with 20 spots to air in all primary dayparts, plus 10 60-second spots, plus the recorded message.

Investigate to see if there are public service announcements (PSAs) available to you on the radio. Should you encounter difficulties in finding spots available, work with a government-funded employment and training program for assistance. Many stations also offer "community bulletin board" listings of job opportunities in the area, many at no cost.

Radio, like television, is often best used as part of a media blitz. Consider combining radio messages with print messages, perhaps to advertise for a recruitment event, such as an open house or career or job fair.

Radio can also be a solution for unique employment needs. Consider Rockwell International in Huntsville, Alabama. The company needed to demonstrate that there was a large number of available professionals in the area as part of the bidding process for a science and engineering contract. Radio was selected as a medium that could quickly reach out, in an intrusive manner, and solicit the response needed from a wide range of industry professionals. A one-month run of three different radio spots elicited about 3,000 applications. The cost for the campaign, including actors, production costs, and purchase of radio time was less than $5,000.[5]

Six Flags Over Georgia, an amusement park with over 4,000 employees, also uses radio to meet its peak hiring needs. Radio is the choice medium, as it can be targeted to a prime-candidate audience wishing to work summers only—those ages 15 to 24.

In one radio campaign Six Flags asked listeners to come to a Six Flags' job fair, which drew 1,000 teenagers. They did not use print advertising for this campaign because of the target audience's age.[6]

IDEA NO. 29: USING DOOR HANGERS, HANDBILLS, AND DIRECT MAIL

Door hangers, handbills, and direct mail have several things in common: they are all intrusive in nature, they can be targeted, and they are relatively low cost—making these excellent recruitment strategies for recruiters today.

Door hangers are messages placed in individuals' paper boxes or literally hung from the front-door knob. They can be hand-delivered individually, or advertisers distribute door-hanger bags containing several coupons and advertisements from a number of different types of advertisers. Recruitment messages on door hangers are generally advertising for low-wage, entry-level positions at retail establishments, where the prospective candidates tend to live close to the work site. Many retailers find that combining recruitment messages with coupons for merchandise/products is another way to cut recruitment costs and entice candidates in two ways. Dairy Queen uses a flyer with part-time shifts listed on one side, with cents-off coupons on the flip side. Kroger uses a short application-type form on one side of a flyer, with a coupon for $3 off at their pharmacy on the other side.

ERA®, the real estate company, used a unique door-hanger type message on July 4. In the wee hours of the morning, small American flags were placed in front of each house in several neighborhoods, with a small recruitment message that read, ''Happy Birthday, America. Our gift to you to help celebrate the 4th.'' Then, in smaller print, they asked, ''Do you know someone who: needs more income? is better than their present job? knows the value of investigating opportunities?'' The message listed a number for interested individuals to call.

Organizations need to consider carefully how they are going to distribute door-hanger messages if undertaking this activity in-house. One employer discovered that the cheaper method was not necessarily the best method, when they hired teenagers to distribute the recruitment messages. The employment office ended up getting calls from angry residents complaining about the teenagers who had tromped through shrub beds, but no calls regarding the recruitment notice!

Handbills are recruitment messages printed on a one-page flyer and are generally handed out to passers-by, placed on car windshields, or distributed at point of sale (placed in a bag of merchandise, handed to customers as they exit). Again, retailers have the most opportunity to utilize this method.

T.J. Maxx, the off-price retailing company, uses this strategy with a flyer that has space for the recruit to complete name, address, phone, and days and times available. Hallmark stores have used an in-store flyer, in the form of a baby announcement (in shades of baby blue and pink). The announcement heralded the opening of a new store in the area and requested interested candidates to apply. Some retailers are also including coupons for merchandise on the same flyer.

Direct mail is more versatile, in that it can be used just as easily by companies without direct customer contact, and can be targeted for entry-level as well as professional, technical, and managerial positions. Direct mail can concentrate on one specific geographic area or can focus on candidates with certain qualifications across a large geographic area.

There are several different ways to use direct mail. One way targets candidates within a geographic area by sending out a message to one zip code or to a series of zip codes. Companies that provide this service send out mailer packages or handle your mailing for you.

Organizations can specifically target direct-mail pieces to a number of audiences by the careful selection of the mailing list. There are a number of ways organizations can use mailing lists at no cost: rosters of clubs and organizations, church directories, school rosters, contact information gathered at an open house or career fair, past applicants, and former employees. Likewise, many avenues are available from which to purchase mailing lists: professional and trade organizations, publications, mailing-list brokers, schools, state and national certification and licensing bureaus, and research companies. To gain more information on mailing lists available, contact your recruitment-advertising agency or look in the phone book yellow pages under *mailing.* You may also want to contact directly the publications with readership you are interested in targeting, as well as clubs and organizations with membership of the targeted audience. You may also source lists through the use of the directory of lists known as *Direct Mail Lists, Rates, and Data,* an SRDS publication and most comprehensive source for lists in the United States.

Mailing lists are generally leased to employers for a one-time use only. Sometimes there are prices for multiple usage. The cost to use a mailing list is priced per thousand names, usually in the $35 to $100 per thousand range, with a minimum fee of $300 to $500. The mailing list can be leased in the form of mailing labels or computer disk. Most mailing lists are "seeded" with bogus names and addresses that are directed back to the mailing-list company to ensure that the user does not mail to the list more than once.

In working with brokers and others leasing these lists, you may select the criteria to be used in the search. For example, you can limit the list to geographic area, educational background, title, size of company, type of company, and even purchase decisions (for example, by candidates who have attended a national conference sponsored by the organization in the past year). By using these "selects," you are able to carefully target your message to only those candidates you wish to reach. Brokers can also let you know, with the criteria you have selected, how many are in that field. For example, you may have selected so many criteria that there is only a small sampling, making the purchase of the list cost-prohibitive. Conversely, you may have not limited the number of candidates adequately, making the mailing list unwieldy. Not all lists are well-maintained, so do your homework and check with other users in making your decision.

Guidelines for Direct Mail

A recruiter attending a seminar was frustrated with direct-mail recruitment. He indicated that his company had been using direct mail for some time, but with increasing numbers of mailers, he wondered how he could get candidates to open, read, and respond to direct mail more effectively.

Recruiters using direct mail can learn from the many advertisers who have studied this marketing concept and learned how to send messages with impact. Here are some of those guidelines:

- First-class mail gets opened before bulk mail. In fact, many large companies with mail departments (and some secretaries) sometimes toss bulk mail in an attempt to cut down on the ''junk'' mail. By sending first class, you also learn how ''clean'' the list is, and can obtain a discount from the mailing-list broker if there are excessive returns (first-class mail that cannot be delivered is returned to the sender).

- Avoid mailing labels, since this looks like an impersonal piece of mail. The better solution is to hand address (this mail gets opened first) or to print the address directly on the envelope (with word processing, this is becoming a reality today).

- Enclose the direct-mail piece in an envelope. This will not only protect the mailer from damage in transit, but will also increase the chances that it is read. A self-mailer (a piece that is folded in half or in thirds) is seen by candidates as being too commercial.

- Personalize the message if possible. Use word processing to include the name of the candidate in the copy.

- Avoid a commercial look. Instead, use a format that looks like a personalized business letter, a party invitation, or a press release, which is better than a format that screams of being an advertisement.

- Make it easy for the ''customer'' to ''buy.'' Include a toll-free 800 number, an employment hot line number, or a 24-hour number so that candidates can call in immediately. Or include a postage-paid reply card that interested candidates can drop in the mail to receive more information, or be contacted for the next steps in the selection process. Business reply permits are inexpensive to purchase; your organization may already have one (check with your mail room, or with marketing or public relations).

Allstate Insurance has found that direct mail is more effective in recruitment of candidates than any other medium. They sent direct-mail messages to customers for positions in a number of areas, including data processing. They had previously used newspaper advertising and received only one or two inquiries. In one direct-mail campaign, they received over 500 calls, which resulted in 20 hires.[7]

IDEA NO. 30: TAPPING INTO CORPORATE AND PUBLIC-ACCESS DATABASES

Recruitment is going high-tech, and many recruiters are investigating strategies that integrate new technologies available into the recruitment function. Database programs that make use of storing and tracking applications and résumés via the computer are becoming a smart way for recruiters to make use of technology today.

Resumes-On-Computer (ROC) is one such product. It is a product offered through the Human Resources Information Network (HRIN). The ROC database contains résumés supplied to the company by some 700 résumé sources, including professional résumé writers, outplacement firms, and quick printing firms. Subscribers to the database service will be able to seek candidates in a wide range of occupations and industries, and can search defined fields such as occupation, industry, education level, years of experience, geographic preference, and posting date.

In addition to ROC, HRIN offers three additional databases accessible to human resources professionals. College Recruitment Database contains 6,000 résumés of graduating undergraduate and graduate students from 21 colleges and universities. Military in Transition Database has over 31,000 active duty and separated military personnel seeking employment. Minority Graduate Database represents students from over 400 schools.[8]

Recruitment Enhancement Services (RES) is a human resource consult-ing company that founded the applicant response management industry in 1984. Not an employment agency or search firm, the company places help-wanted ads for their clients. The ads contain a toll-free 800 number for candidates to use, and the company interviews candidates to capture key information, which is entered into the computer system. Client companies receive information back from RES via computer disk. Advertisements can be run without company identification, should a confidential response be desired. RES also offers the software for sale to companies.

CORS (Corporate Organizing and Research Services) has also devel-oped a software program for client companies. Called CORSLINK, it per-mits companies to computerize current résumés and applications, as well as integrating search assignments completed by CORS (see the section in this chapter on research agencies).

There are at least five major categories of recruitment databases, based upon the group responsible for maintaining the system. There are those maintained by university alumni groups, employment agencies, and executive-search firms; those open to the public and maintained by private companies; and corporate job banks. A listing of contact information for these banks is included in the Appendix.

In deciding whether or not to use a database, consider these issues:

- The size of the database.
- Ease of use of the system.
- Source of résumé information.
- Screening process for résumé input.
- Frequency of system update.
- Confidentiality of listings.
- Cost of use, including hidden user fees.
- Method of contact with candidate.[9]

IDEA NO. 31: USING RESEARCH AGENCIES, "VIDEO" AGENCIES, AND OTHER "NEW" AGENCIES

There are a number of alternatives to traditional recruitment agencies—those agencies that search for qualified candidates for a fee. One new breed of agency includes those providing research services. These companies own or tap into vast databases of names, addresses, phone numbers, job titles, responsibilities, and other pertinent information on prospective candidates. You provide the general job requirements, such as years of experience, level of education, type of degree, kind of position held; and the research company provides you with a list of candidates who meet those specifications. CORS, Corporate Organizing and Research Services, Inc., located in Itasca, Illinois, is such a company. The organization, in addition to providing names and contact information, will make initial calls and prescreen candidates to determine interest and compatibility. Bay Research Group, Inc., based in Rockford, Illinois, also provides a variety of recruitment research services. There are now over 150 similar firms selling résumé databases in the United States.[10]

"Video" agencies are those that provide a unique service often needed by companies searching for individuals across the country. With this service, the employer advertises for the position, receives responses, and screens candidates for those most interested in interviewing. These candidates, most of whom are located out of town, are then contacted by the agency, which sets up an interview. The interview follows a structured format, with the interview questions already selected in advance by the employer, to be used for all candidates. The agency tapes the candidates during the interview and sends videos to the employer to review and select the candidates.

By using this service, recruiters can save on travel costs for either flying the candidates to the corporate headquarters, or the travel costs and time involved in the recruiter interviewing candidates at their home base.

As long as a structured interview format is used for all candidates being considered, this type of selection process is entirely permissible for affirmative-action purposes. However, care should be taken to ensure strict conformity to a structured interview format, since there is documentation of the interview process that could be used as evidence if a claim of discrimination is filed.

Other "new" agencies are hatching across the country, providing new services needed by recruiters today. For example, some agencies can act as an extension of your human resources department and conduct the entire search for you. They may present one to three candidates for the company to interview. These companies offer low fees, generally in the 3- to 7-percent range. These companies can charge a lower-than-traditional fee because they receive their payment in advance and are acting exclusively in the search.

Some relatively new agencies are working exclusively with certain industries and occupations, such as health-care occupations, or hard-to-fill entry-level positions, such as retail and foodservice workers. They are often very effective, in that they understand the industry and the occupation and have an excellent network from which to recruit qualified candidates. These agencies also offer affordable fee arrangements, usually for providing multiple hires.

Even if your organization has traditionally not used recruitment agencies, investigate these new services, as they may be quite affordable and effective in meeting your employment needs.

IDEA NO. 32: ADVERTISING ON BILLBOARDS—CINEMA, HIGHWAY, PORTABLE, AND SPORTS

Be creative in placing recruitment messages where people will see them, and where other products and services are already being marketed successfully. Why not consider highway bulletin boards, as well as portable and sports bulletin boards to creatively place recruitment messages.

Highway bulletin boards can receive high visibility, especially those seen by your prospective candidate, perhaps on the way to and from work. One employer uses their location as a recruitment tool and communicates this advantage on a highway bulletin board that says, "If you worked here, your commute would be over."

Bulletin board messages must be short and to the point, using bold graphics to capture the interest of the driver. Readers should be given some action to take: a number to call or a person to contact for more information.

Employers can also use portable bulletin boards to publicize a recruitment event, such as an open house, career fair, or information seminar. They might even be used to communicate where interested candidates can apply when a new facility is opening.

Sports bulletin boards are the large electronic messages that advertisers purchase during sporting events. Since you have a captive audience, consider if this audience is one you want to reach with your recruitment message.

Cinema billboard offers another way to reach prospective candidates. These are the advertisements that are shown to advertise for sodas, popcorn, candy, and even recruitment opportunities before the movie begins. Generally, advertisers develop a slide with the message to be used. Since it is only one slide, the message must be brief, using bold graphics and colors to capture the attention of the viewer. When you purchase this advertising space, you receive a specific number of showings of the slide before each movie, and if it is a multiple-movie house, it is shown before each movie. You can buy advertising in weekly or monthly increments.

IDEA NO. 33: RECRUITING VIA AIRPLANE BANNERS

''Airplane banners for recruitment messages—you've got to be kidding,'' you may be thinking. Recruitment messages are literally being seen anywhere there has been traditional marketing for other goods and services.

Some employers are finding that they have a perfect captive audience at the beach or at sporting events. Using airplane banners is an inexpensive way to raise awareness about employment opportunities in a fun way.

Keep your message short—you don't have many letters to use to let people know what you have to offer!

IDEA NO. 34: USING KIOSKS

Kiosks are the large, often back-lit advertising displays seen in airports and shopping malls, often freestanding. Traditionally they have been used to advertise hotels, restaurants, and airlines within airports, and to advertise retail establishments, banks, insurance companies, and hospitals in shopping malls. Today, recruitment messages are appearing on this medium.

You can select kiosk locations to target the population you need to reach. Airport kiosks will reach the business traveler; mall kiosks will reach different ages and ethnic populations, based upon the location of the shopping center. Generally, the mall office can provide you with demographic information that will be helpful in selecting the appropriate kiosk location, or you can call upon your recruitment-advertising agency.

One employer targeted a shopping center with an older shopper population to place a message targeted to attract older workers. They used an applicant-reply card in a holder attached to the kiosk to encourage candidates to respond, and to track response rates.

The Children's Hospital in Boston targeted a younger population with a recruitment theme, "Your Work Will Be Remembered All Their Lives," depicting a nurse caring for a young child. The ads cost $2,400 each for a six-month time period, and were rotated every two weeks among the kiosk locations within the mall. Deane Coady, employment manager for the hospital, was pleased with the results. Many "hotline" calls were received, and visibility was enhanced within the community.[11]

IDEA NO. 35: POINT-OF-SALE ADVERTISING—COUNTER CARDS, POSTERS, READERBOARD, CASH-REGISTER RECEIPTS, TRAY LINERS, AND OTHER MESSAGES

Point of sale (POS), also called point of purchase (POP), is a time which many organizations with direct customer contact are utilizing to capture the interest of would-be applicants. T.J. Maxx uses a one-page flyer, displayed on check-out counters, with the message, "And you thought all we offered was the hottest name brand fashions at 20–60 percent off," with a miniapplication at the bottom. The flyer asks candidates to apply in person or fill out the coupon and mail it to the locations listed.

One bookstore used a bookmark at the point of sale, with the message:

This is a bookmark. Or is it? You could certainly use it as a bookmark and we'd be delighted. We'd also be delighted if you turned it over, filled in the information, and mailed it back to us to apply for one of our store manager, assistant manager, or other available positions.

The back of the bookmark contained space for interested individuals to supply name, address, phone number, and other pertinent information.[12]

E&B Marine, a company that sells boating supplies and accessories via catalog, uses a unique opportunity to recruit candidates. Within the pages of its catalog is a recruitment message, stating, "You can get everything at E&B, EVEN A GREAT JOB!" The catalog supplies a coupon for candidates to complete and mail in and includes a toll-free number.

Retailers can also use a variety of methods to advertise to customers, including messages on cash-register receipts, tray liners (in fast-food restaurants), counter cards, readerboard signs, and other in-store messages. One video rental shop sends recruitment messages home to customers inside the rented video tape.

For those companies using POS messages, make sure that you are not communicating an inadvertent message to customers that you won't be able to provide them with the service they need because you are short-staffed. Make sure that recruitment messages are upbeat and positive. Don't imply through your message that anyone will be hired. One employer used the message, ''Place your name on our employment waiting list'' to present this image.

IDEA NO. 36: USING CORPORATE NEWSLETTERS

Why not use your corporate newsletter to send out the message of the positions that are open within your organization. Not only is this a great way to communicate the message to current employees about job openings for which they could apply, but it is also a good way to remind employees of your employee-referral program (see Chapter Six on designing employee-referral programs).

Remember, too, that there is a pass-along market—family members and friends who may also read the publication. You may be able to reach a number of candidates by using this low-cost/no-cost medium.

IDEA NO. 37: FAXING RECRUITMENT INFORMATION

Many recruiters are taking advantage of the new telecommunications equipment accessible to most candidates today and are using this as part of their recruitment schemes. Some employers are offering the fax, or facsimile machine, to receive résumés and other response data from interested candidates. It permits candidates to send information immediately without having to wait for the mail service, or hand-deliver application information.

IDEA NO. 38: TAPING AUDIO AND VIDEO RECRUITMENT CASSETTES

Candidates today want to be entertained, and recruiters are delivering with innovative formats for recruitment messages. Audio and video presents a new, exciting format for recruitment messages, and can be used in unique ways.

Instead of using letters and invitations to targeted candidates via direct mail, some employers are taping their recruitment message on audio or video tape, inviting the candidate to play the message and see what's in store. The taped message can be an invitation to a recruitment event such as an open house, career fair, or information seminar, or can suggest that the candidate call for additional information.

Video and audio tapes can also provide excellent follow-up messages with information on the company, the community, and other pertinent information that may be of interest to the candidate and the candidate's family, especially if a relocation is in the picture.

Video can be used as part of career-fair and open-house attractions as a means to communicate company and job information to interested candidates. Video can also help develop a positive image before on-campus recruitment, as used by one high-tech employer. They developed a lively music video format to entice college students to consider Wang as a potential employer.[13]

Hardee's Food Systems has developed specific videos for each of its programs targeted at distinctive labor-market segments. ''New Horizons'' for older workers, ''FastTracks'' for teen workers, and ''CAPABILITIES'' for persons with disabilities each have a companion video, which can be used at any number of recruitment events, from career fairs and open houses, to information seminars. Each of these videos can also be used when recruiters call on programs providing employment services to these groups.

IDEA NO. 39: CUSTOMER-REFERRAL PROGRAMS

In restaurants or retail stores, it is perfectly acceptable to recruit customers as employees. However, in other businesses such as manufacturers or distributors, it is not appropriate to recruit your customer since they may not appreciate your taking away their employees and could retaliate by taking away their business. Therefore, in this situation, why not consider a customer-referral program. Similar in nature to an employee-referral program, you provide some sort of incentive such as cash, prizes, or even a product or service you provide, when a referral is hired.

Use the guidelines for implementing an employee-referral program with customers, and remember to handle this strategy with kid gloves—these are your customers, after all!

IDEA NO. 40: DEVELOPING DESKTOP RECRUITING

Since many college students are computer-literate, and may be bombarded by a number of conventional recruitment activities, Squibb Corp. decided to take a slightly different approach and developed a recruitment diskette targeted at graduating M.B.A. students. The program was an interactive one, using humor, interesting and unusual graphics, case studies, and a menu full of options for information.

Students could choose from a menu selection of Squibb history, the M.B.A. and Squibb, the Squibb matrix, M.B.A. classifieds, and other information. Students can jump from one part of the menu to another or can go through an entire menu item if desired.

Squibb Corp. sent the disks to students attending Harvard University, Yale University, and other prestigious business schools. Most of the diskettes were mailed to some 1,000 Harvard candidates.

Cost for the development of the program was $35,000, plus the costs for duplicating and mailing the disks. Squibb found through a follow-up questionnaire that 33 percent viewed the program once; 29 percent viewed it twice; 18 percent viewed it three times or more. Squibb was pleased with the results and felt that the use of the disks was one of many important factors in their recruitment campaign.[14]

Ideas for Nontraditional Recruiting Activities

Idea No. 25: Telemarketing (telerecruiting).

Idea No. 26: Direct recruitment.

Idea No. 27: Using television—major network commercials, cable advertising, and public service announcements (PSAs).

Idea No. 28: Advertising on the radio, and combining print with radio.

Idea No. 29: Using door hangers, handbills, and direct mail.

Idea No. 30: Tapping into corporate and public-access databases.

Idea No. 31: Using research agencies, ''video'' agencies, and other ''new'' agencies.

Idea No. 32: Advertising on billboards—cinema, highway, portable, and sports.

Idea No. 33: Recruiting via airplane banners.

Idea No. 34: Using kiosks.

Idea No. 35: Point-of-sale advertising—counter cards, posters, readerboard, cash-register receipts, tray liners, and other messages.

Idea No. 36: Using corporate newsletters.

Idea No. 37: Faxing recruitment information.

Idea No. 38: Taping audio and video recruitment cassettes.

Idea No. 39: Customer-referral programs.

Idea No. 40: Developing desktop recruiting.

Ideas for Nontraditional Recruiting Activities

Idea	Cost	Number People	Lead Time	Target
Idea No. 25: Telemarketing	L–H	M	M–L	Y
Idea No. 26: Direct recruitment	L	—	S	Y
Idea No. 27: Television	L–H	M	M–L	Y
Idea No. 28: Radio	L–H	M	M–L	Y
Idea No. 29: Door hangers, etc.	L–H	—	M–L	Y
Idea No. 30: Databases	M–H	—	M–L	Y
Idea No. 31: Agencies	M–H	—	M–L	Y
Idea No. 32: Billboards	M–H	M	M–L	Y
Idea No. 33: Airplane banners	M–H	M	M–L	Y
Idea No. 34: Kiosk	M–H	M	M–L	Y
Idea No. 35: Point-of-sale ads	L–H	M	M–L	N
Idea No. 36: Newsletters	L	—	M–L	N
Idea No. 37: Faxing information	L	—	S	N
Idea No. 38: Audio/video tapes	M–H	M	M–L	Y
Idea No. 39: Customer referrals	L–H	M	M–L	N
Idea No. 40: Desktop recruiting	H	M	L	Y

Key:
Cost   Lead time
  Low   0–$200   Short   0–1 week
  Medium $200–$1,000   Moderate   1 week–4 weeks
  High $1,000+   Long   4+ weeks
Number people   Target
  Single   1   Yes
  Multiple   2 or more   No
  Either

ENDNOTES

1. Catherine D. Fyock, *The Hiring Handbook* (Greenvale, N.Y.: 1988), Institute for Management, pp. 86–88.

2. Linda Stockman Vines, ''Recruiting Outlook,'' *Human Resource Executive,* October 1989, p. 23.

3. Linda Fernandez, *Now Hiring* (Washington, D.C.: 1989), Bureau of National Affairs, pp. 210–211.

4. Tim Chauran, ''Prime Time for Televised Recruitment,'' *Recruitment Today,* May/June 1989, p. 53.

5. Jennifer J. Koch, "Applicants Tune in to Radio," *Recruitment Today*, Fall 1989, pp. 7–10.

6. Ibid., pp. 10–12.

7. Allan Halcrow, "You're in Good Hands with Direct Mail," *Recruitment Today*, February/March 1989, pp. 21–22.

8. "Recruiting Made Easy: HRIN's Newest Résumé Database," *HR Update*, February 1991, pp. 2–3.

9. Rod Willis, "Recruitment: Playing the Database Game," *Personnel*, May 1990, p. 25.

10. Ibid., pp. 25–29.

11. Jennifer J. Koch, "Strong Medicine for Health Care Recruiters," *Recruitment Today*, Spring 1990, pp. 18–19.

12. "Focus," *Recruitment Today*, July 1989, p. 58.

13. Jennifer J. Koch, "Why Video?" *Recruitment Today*, Spring 1990, pp. 30–34.

14. Jennifer J. Koch, "Desktop Recruiting," *Recruitment Today*, Winter 1990, pp. 32–37.

Chapter Four

Expanding New Geographic Boundaries

M ost employers can clearly illustrate the geographic boundaries from which they recruit each position. For many entry-level positions, the boundaries are small and centered within the neighborhood. Employers can fill middle-management and technical and professional positions by attracting candidates from a regional, and sometimes a national, base, depending upon the scarcity of qualified candidates; they usually recruit top-management candidates on a national basis.

For every employer, there is probably some way to redefine the geographic boundaries for recruitment when a creative approach is applied. This chapter will explore some new ways to attract candidates from new places.

IDEA NO. 41: RELOCATION OPTIONS

Why not recruit where you have a distinct recruitment advantage? DCH Regional Medical Center in Tuscaloosa, Alabama, did just that with an advertisement placed in *Southern Living* magazine. The ad shows a four-color picture of a beautiful country lane; a woman is riding a bicycle down the quiet road, with a child in the basket behind her, and a dog following along beside her. The caption reads, "If you want to work in one of America's most advanced hospitals, you'll have to get used to the traffic." The ad goes on to entice candidates with this ad copy:

Whoever said you couldn't have it all, didn't work for us.
If you want a life where there's room to breathe, you'll find it here.
If you want a career where you work with some of the most advanced medical technology in the country, you'll find that, too.

The ad concludes with the statement:

Our medicine will challenge you, but it's our countryside that rewards you. The heart of Alabama, surrounded by the best of the South.
You'll find a whole new career opportunity that's off the beaten path. So to speak.

Employers need to look at their own geographic advantages and use them in the recruitment strategy. For example, an employer located in the warm, sunny South might want to develop beautiful recruitment messages depicting the delightful climate and use these ads in the Northeast during cold, snowy winter months. Employers located in a healthy economic community might consider recruitment activities in areas of high unemployment, selling candidates on the wisdom of such a move.

Employers may also want to target those places where organizations are closing their doors for business or downsizing. Nationwide Advertising Service, Inc. offers their clients information on high-tech layoffs, for example, in the form of a newsletter. Employers may want to target recruitment activities in these communities through open houses and other recruitment events. Many employers are contacting these businesses directly and working with outplacement counselors and human resource professionals to recruit laid-off employees.

An employer located within suburbia may actively recruit candidates close to home, offering a short commute time as a distinct employment advantage. Likewise, city employers may find that stressing the benefits of being close to the city and city activities can be a great positioning for some candidates.

For employers looking to relocate candidates, there may be increased resistance, with increasing numbers of dual-career couples. To attract and relocate candidates, employers are sweetening the pot to entice individuals to take the move to the new location. For example, they are asking realtors, as well as corporate relocation departments, to provide more services, such as spouse-relocation assistance and family-adjustment programs as part of their packages of services for relocating employees.

IDEA NO. 42: WELCOME WAGON

One target market to consider is the family members of relocating individuals. Spouses, as well as the extended family of children and in-laws, may also be relocating with the individual and may need employment.

Why not target this market through a direct method—the neighborhood Welcome Wagon or Newcomers group. Let these groups know of your recruitment needs, and provide them with recruitment materials to be distributed to relocating family members.

One retailer, already working with the local Welcome Wagon, coupled a recruitment message with their product message (which included discount coupons) to entice potential employees to visit their establishment and check out the employment opportunities at the same time.

IDEA NO. 43: MASS-TRANSIT ADVERTISING

Mass transit offers a wide range of reasonable alternatives to attracting candidates. Advertising can take the form of signs on the inside and outside of buses, trains, and subways, and inside of mass-transit terminals and waiting stations.

Word Processors Personnel Service in Washington, D.C., used a recruitment message on fare cards used by mass-transit commuters. The fare cards said, ''One of Washington's top employers is looking for you!'' The card highlighted the types of positions for which they were seeking candidates for both temporary and permanent placement, with a message to call today, followed by the phone number. The office is located near one of the station entrances.

In Boston, several employers have used mass transit with outstanding results. United Airlines targeted immigrants in their ads, with a caption, ''Get a job at Logan and we'll offer you the world.'' After bullets, which listed the benefits of employment, the ad provided a number to call for information. As a result of this campaign, they filled all open positions and generated a backlog of 200 applicants.[1]

The Bank of Boston attracted temporary workers for a new temporary pool. The subway posters cost $25,000 for a three-month campaign, but in-house savings amounted to over $1 million.[2]

Talbots used transit advertising to fill over 360 positions for personal shoppers during an eight-month period. Posters contained a tear-off information coupon to make it easy for candidates to apply.[3]

One employer used mass-transit advertising as a means to attract large numbers of candidates for its operations in the Atlanta, Georgia, market. The organization placed ads inside buses and trains in the MARTA system, with a take-home coupon offered. Advertisements included both recruitment and product messages, so the human resources department was able to share budget dollars with marketing/advertising budgets.

The ads ran for three months at a time, with up to 50 applications mailed in each day. The organization was not always ready for the large response rate and found that just keeping up with the applicant tracking was a huge task. Further, candidates tended to be those who didn't have their own transportation, so they needed to be placed in those locations near bus and train lines.

IDEA NO. 44: TRANSPORTATION OPTIONS

What happens when there are candidates out there that want to work for you, but can't because they must rely on public transportation—and you're not near a bus or train line? Many employers are thinking creatively in solving this problem.

One solution is to offer transportation in-house, busing employees from the end point of the mass-transit system to the employment location. Others are paying for cab service to and from this location. Still others have banded together to offer shared transportation, such as the "burger bus" in Richmond, Virginia, that takes inner-city employees to their place of employment (often in the service industry) located well outside of the city limits in suburban Richmond.

Some employer groups have gone together to petition for public transportation to be provided to their suburban locations as a means to attract and retain employees.

IDEA NO. 45: RELOCATION SERVICE PROVIDERS

Realtors, especially those with large in-house corporate relocation services departments, may be able to be recruiters for your organization. Often, these realtors are expected to provide spouse/family career assistance for family members of the relocated executive or mid-manager. Let these realtors know of your employment needs, and network with them to discover a source of candidates entering your community.

IDEA NO. 46: HOUSING

No employer wants the added expense of providing housing for employees; however, it may be a necessity for some organizations located in isolated places. On the island of Hawaii, for example, resort employers are forced to provide housing through a mandate from the County of Hawaii. Here, the high cost of living, small numbers of residents, isolated location, and severe housing shortage compound recruitment problems.

The Royal Waikoloan constructed housing units within their hotel village, with 300 acres of land made available for future development. The Mauna Lani Bay Hotel, with 10 percent vacancy rates at all times, built 225 housing units nearby for their 700 employes.[4]

Cedar Point, a seasonal amusement park located in Sandusky, Ohio, provides housing for over two thirds of its summer employees ages 18 and over who live over 25 miles from the park. Both dormitory and apartment-style housing—all multiple occupancy—is offered on a first-come, first-served basis. Employees receive a complete handbook that outlines the procedures, policies, and guidelines for living in these accommodations.

IDEA NO. 47: BUSING

Atlanta is one city whose public transportation system does not go where many new jobs are—in the extreme northern parts of the city. Some employers, such as Temp Force Temporaries, offer transportation in an attempt to attract workers who otherwise could not get to work.[5]

There are a myriad of difficulties in developing a busing program, such as finding an employee reliable enough to serve as driver, for starters! There are also liability issues and cost issues, which often make this avenue difficult to orchestrate. However, it is an option when you are faced with the choice of providing busing or having no employees!

Employers in the Lake Buena Vista area, near Walt Disney World, find it difficult, if not impossible, to attract employees. The area surrounding the Disney property is inundated with restaurants, hotels, and motels, and very few residential areas. Many employers here must provide transportation as a competitive edge.

IDEA NO. 48: OVER-THE-ROAD (OTR) TRUCKS

Have you seen the recruitment messages on the back of over-the-road trucks? They ask drivers to consider the opportunities of this occupation, offering a number to call for more information. In your business, do you have a similar opportunity to send messages to candidates?

IDEA NO. 49: MOBILE RECRUITING VANS

When the candidates can't or won't come to you, why not take recruitment to the candidates? Many employers are doing just that through the use of mobile recruiting vans. An employer can purchase vans for such a purpose (and use them to bus employees if need be), or can lease or rent the vans from a local car-rental company for a specific occasion.

One employer used a recruitment van in conjunction with the sponsorship of a rap concert. The employer located a recruitment van in the parking lot as a means to attract young people to summer and part-time jobs. Another employer rented a van to tempt summer vacationers at a beach sand-castle contest sponsored by the community to stay for the year.

An employer can use vans in conjunction with events, or to highlight participation at career fairs or on-campus recruiting days. Vans can be an excellent method to entice job candidates to apply when opening a new facility. The employer can locate the van at the building site so that applications can be taken on-the-spot.

Little Caesar Enterprises, Inc. advertises for their van appearance through the use of an ad, depicting a line drawing of the van, driven by the cartoon character seen in their product commercials. The van says, "Great jobs available," and the ad begins by asking readers to "stop by our van! van!" (similar to their "pizza! pizza!" advertising theme).

Ideas for Expanding Geographic Boundaries

Idea No. 41: Relocation options.

Idea No. 42: Welcome Wagon.

Idea No. 43: Mass-transit advertising.

Idea No. 44: Transportation options.

Idea No. 45: Relocation service providers.

Idea No. 46: Housing.

Idea No. 47: Busing.

Idea No. 48: Over-the-road (OTR) trucks.

Idea No. 49: Mobile recruiting vans.

Ideas for Expanding Geographic Boundaries

Idea	Cost	Number People	Lead Time	Target
Idea No. 41: Relocation options	M–H	—	M–L	N
Idea No. 42: Welcome Wagon	L–M	M	M–L	N
Idea No. 43: Mass-transit ads	M–H	M	M–L	Y
Idea No. 44: Transportation	H	M	M–L	N
Idea No. 45: Realtors	L	—	M–L	N
Idea No. 46: Housing	H	M	M–L	N
Idea No. 47: Busing	H	M	M–L	N
Idea No. 48: Over-the-road (OTR) trucks	M–H	M	M–L	N
Idea No. 49: Recruiting vans	L–H	M	M–L	N

Key:
Cost
  Low   0–$200
  Medium $200–$1,000
  High $1,000+
Number people
  Single   1
  Multiple 2 or more
  Either
Lead time
  Short   0–1 week
  Moderate 1 week–4 weeks
  Long   4+ weeks
Target
  Yes
  No

ENDNOTES

1. Tim Chauran, "Get High Mileage from Your Advertising Dollar," *Recruitment Today,* February/March 1989, pp. 48–51.
2. Ibid.
3. Ibid.
4. Margaret Magnus, "Publisher's Letter," *Recruitment Today,* Summer 1990, p. 3.
5. Aaron Bernstein, Richard W. Anderson, and Wendy Zellner, "Help Wanted," *Business Week,* August 10, 1987, p. 53.

Chapter Five

Developing and Implementing Updated Approaches: The Newspaper

I n many labor markets today, the formerly "tried and true" methods of attracting job candidates are no longer as effective in meeting staffing goals. One traditional method of finding candidates has been placing help-wanted advertising in the classified or display sections of the daily metro newspaper. However, to do effective recruiting, employers must examine some nontraditional approaches in today's difficult labor markets to reach that potential employee who is not actively seeking employment.

IDEA NO. 50: USING RECRUITMENT-ADVERTISING AGENCIES

Recruitment-advertising agencies work with their clients to create and place recruitment advertisements. The advantage of working with an ad agency is that they do the homework on creating recruitment ads and charge their clients a nominal fee for these services. Most recruitment-advertising agencies receive the bulk of their income from commissions they receive from newspapers, similar to the way in which travel agencies receive commission from the airlines.

There are large agencies with creative staffs and smaller agencies with one or two staff members who do it all. Some agencies are national in scope, some are regionally focused, and others serve a local clientele.

How does an organization make the decision as to which agency to use? Here are some questions to consider when selecting an agency:

1. **How creative are they?** Have you seen samples of their work? Many organizations request that recruitment agencies prepare a "mini" campaign as part of the bidding process so they can see how the agency will handle their account.

2. **What services do they provide?** Can they give you a listing of direct-mail resources? Do they know of alternative advertising avenues? Can they do in-house research for specific projects? Match the services that are needed with the services offered—don't get carried away and eliminate a smaller agency with fewer services that can meet your needs most effectively.

3. **What is the fee structure for services?** Advertising agencies are not created equally, and some provide services at little or no additional fee, including creative work and ad placement research. However, some agencies will charge for these services, so be sure to clarify before initiating a relationship.

4. **What is the lead time for delivering services?** How responsive can the agency be to your needs? Explore what time frames will be needed to meet space deadlines.

5. **Do you like the people you'll be dealing with?** Have you met them? One human resource professional had the unfortunate experience of being "wowed" by an outstanding agency presentation, only to find later that the sales staff that had been so impressive would not be the individuals handling the account.

6. **Is the agency centralized or decentralized?** There can be many benefits—and pitfalls—in working with an agency with multiple locations. If your organization has multiple sites that will be working with the agency, a decentralized agency with several locations may appeal to the local organizations, which can communicate on a face-to-face basis with the agency, and which feel that the local agency understands the unique recruitment issues within the community. However, not all national agencies with local offices offer the same level of services with the same level of professionalism. Meet with each location you will be working with to ensure uniformity of services and professionalism.

7. **Will your organization be a big account for the agency, or will your account be considered "small potatoes"?** Many recruiters will testify that it is essential for the agency to feel that your business is an important account to them, or else you will be treated

with benign neglect. Determine the amount and size of the agencies' competitive accounts to determine just how "hungry" they are for your business.

Look for recruitment advertising agencies by looking in your local yellow pages. Talk with recruiters from other organizations to see whom they use, and whom they like to work with. Or look at the advertising in human resource publications for national advertising agencies.

In selecting an agency, request that several make a presentation to your organization. Ask that they prepare a minicampaign so that you can get an understanding of their approach and philosophy, and see if there is a match with your business needs. Be sure to check references before making the final decision to see if they deliver on their promises.

In establishing the initial relationship with the agency, spend some time to ensure their understanding of the position responsibilities and requirements, the criteria for successful job candidates, elements of corporate culture, and past recruitment efforts—both successes and failures. Have the agency staff meet with recruiters as well as line managers with hiring responsibilities.

Next, request that the agency prepare some detailed information on their ideas for a recruitment campaign. Inform them of your recruitment budget, specific needs, time frames, and other pertinent data. Ask them to prepare a recruitment action plan for the year.

In working with your recruitment-advertising agency, provide ongoing feedback to let them know what is working and what isn't producing the kind of results you expect. Let them know when they aren't living up to your expectations, or when they aren't being as creative as you want them to be. As with any other business relationship, establish the groundwork for two-way communications that keeps the agency's work on-track.

One warning: be on the lookout for a small group of dishonest agencies who try to trick you into paying for services they did not provide. Here's how the scam works: you have a job opening, and you run an ad yourself in the paper. Later, your accounts payable department receives a tear sheet, showing the ad, with an invoice enclosed. In small print, the invoice says that this is the cost *if* they should run the ad, but everything else about this mailing implies that they have already completed authorized work for you. Be sure to verify and approve all invoices, and alert your accounts payable department so that you avoid being caught in this deceptive practice.

IDEA NO. 51: LOOK TO OTHER SECTIONS OF THE NEWSPAPER

When you advertise in the help-wanted section of the newspaper, you only reach those candidates who are unemployed or very unhappy in their current job, and you fail to reach the candidate you may most want to reach—the candidate who is happily employed someplace else. Instead, position advertising in sections where people are browsing every day.

Consider who your potential employee is and where your potential job candidate is reading the paper. If you are targeting women who are returning to the workplace, why not consider the food sections? One retailer found that placing ads near the grocery store ads on coupon days was effective in attracting this target market. Further, the retailer enhanced the ad by making it in the form of a coupon, so that the applicant could complete the basic information, clip, and mail! This increased response rates because it did not mandate the receipt of a prepared résumé. Remember, only those individuals who are actively seeking employment have prepared résumés!

Several agencies looking to attract older workers found that placing advertisements near the obituary section was effective, because that's where these individuals are reading the paper each day!

To attract attention, ROP (or "run on press") ads—those ads that appear in alternate sections of the paper— must be large enough to stand out on the page with other ads. The small, miniscule ads that used to be found in the classified section are a thing of the past for most employers fighting for their share of the job market. However, many employers are finding that ROP advertising can be as cost-effective, if not more so, than other display-type ads. Also, effective ROP ads use white space and other graphics to gain attention. Notice that the ad in Figure 5–1 for Applebee's uses headlines, white space, and graphics to compete for attention on the page.

Some papers do not yet permit ROP help-wanted ads; however, with the volume of newspaper advertising on the decline overall, it is likely that increasing numbers of papers will permit this type advertising.

IDEA NO. 52: USE OTHER NEWSPAPERS

Investigate small community newspapers or weekly classified publications and bargain shoppers, such as the *Thrifty Nickel*, the *Penny Pincher*, and

FIGURE 5–1
ROP Ads Use Headlines, Graphics, and White Space to Compete for the
Reader's Attention

Source: Courtesy Applebee's/Marcus Restaurants and Bentley, Barnes & Lynn Advertising, Inc.

Bargain Mart for recruitment advertising. You can target specific market segments and geographic areas efficiently, often with substantial savings in the cost of advertising space over major publications.

Many bargain-shopper publications are developing specific help-wanted sections to appeal to the growing interest among employers looking for low-cost alternatives to metro paper advertising. One such publication is the *CareerMart*, a section of the Harte-Hanks *PennySaver* in southern California. The publication offers employers high readership in targeted geographic markets (with a publicized 76 percent readership by south California residents, as opposed to 46 percent for the *L.A. Times*). A new feature is Ad-A-Voice, which permits candidates to call in on an employment hot line for specific job information. The program further permits employers who select the option to have job candidates record their message back to the organization.

Ethnic and community newspapers can be an excellent means to reach minority candidates, as well as candidates from outlying geographic areas. Often, advertising rates in these publications are quite reasonable.

High school, college, and vocational school newspapers provide an option for the employer wishing to target this market. Don't overlook the potential of church newsletters, club and professional organization papers, and other small publications to reach your prospective job candidate.

IDEA NO. 53: TRY DISPLAY ADVERTISING

Display advertisements are those ads typically found in the last section of the help-wanted ads. In some papers, these ads are located in a separate section. Display ads can also be the larger ads found in ROP advertising.

For those organizations that have traditionally relied on classified ads to attract candidates, many are reporting that display advertising, while more expensive on a per-ad basis, is often worth the extra money because of the quantity and quality of candidates responding. Employers are increasingly discovering that paying more for a display ad that brings in larger numbers of qualified candidates is less expensive than paying little for a small classified ad that results in few responses and no hires.

Obviously, if you are currently successfully using classified advertising—spending small amounts on small ads to gain the results that you need—by all means continue to do what's working! There is no need to reinvent the wheel when the wheel is meeting your needs!

IDEA NO. 54: TRY CLASSIFIED ADS!

For those employers relying on display ads only, try the smaller classified ads to determine if a different target audience is reading. One human resources manager was embarking on a particularly difficult assignment for a mid-level accountant, with no respondents from display advertising. However, on a lark, the manager switched the display to classified, and a small number of qualified responses were received, allowing the position to be filled. Sometimes it is difficult, if not impossible, to predict human behavior and response to advertising!

IDEA NO. 55: EXPERIMENTING WITH BLIND ADVERTISING AND THE OMISSION OF CORPORATE LOGOS

If your organization is a nationally known employer with an excellent reputation, you know that your image as an employer works to your advantage in attracting top candidates. However, if you have a poor image as an employer, if your industry suffers from a bad reputation, or if certain occupations for which you recruit are seen as low-status jobs, then your company's image works against you.

While working with Kentucky Fried Chicken, I found that we often did not get a high response rate to our ads—and often that response rate was of a poor quality. In investigating the problem with our recruitment advertising agency, we guessed that many top candidates were not responding to the ad because of the fast-food industry's reputation as an employer. Yet we had generally used the corporate logo in recruitment ads because of the reputation of "chicken done right" with the Colonel. It occurred to us that the bold use of the logo was counterproductive; candidates did not apply with us because of how good a product or service was offered; they applied when they thought of us as a good place to work.

As a result, we discontinued the use of the logo in our recruitment ads. And, subsequently, our response rates increased dramatically, with not just a larger number of responses, but also a higher calibre candidate. The ads eventually let the candidate know who we were in the body of the ad copy, but did not shout out that information until the reader was "hooked" by the advertising message. In fact, many candidates told us that they would normally have never considered fast-food positions, but did so because of this ad. Organizations with an exceptionally outstanding reputation as an employer may find the opposite as being true: whenever they place an ad in the paper which identifies them as the employer, they receive mountains of résumés and applications. One such employer is Federal Express, having a superior reputation throughout the country. When they place an ad in the paper, they often receive hundreds of responses. And, being the thoughtful employer that they are, they want to respond to each résumé, which can be an overwhelming task.

For these organizations, a blind ad—one which does not identify the name of the employer and asks candidates to respond to a post office box—may be an appropriate alternative. Typically, blind advertising dramatically reduces response rates for the primary reason that candidates don't know with whom they are applying—and fear that the organization might be their own!

Blind ads may also be appropriate for a number of other reasons in addition to response reduction, including:

- Maintaining security when an employee is being terminated and the organization is beginning the search for a replacement.
- Determining the approximate lead time needed to begin a search for a top-level executive, prior to the need.
- Adding one specific position, or replacing one employee, in the midst of an organizational layoff.

Be aware that blind ads do tend to reduce response rates among candidates who are currently successfully working elsewhere, and that potentially excellent candidates may not apply because of the blind ad approach. Use blind ads with caution when appropriate situations arise.

IDEA NO. 56: INSTALLING OR LISTING AN 800 TELEPHONE NUMBER

In order to make it easy for the candidate who is currently employed (and doesn't have a prepared résumé—and doesn't have time to prepare one, either) to respond to your advertisement, why not install an 800 toll-free number to permit job candidates to explore the opportunity with you. This is an excellent way to entice that person who is just "browsing" the ads to respond quickly and easily, permitting you to capitalize on that "impulse" buy (in the terms of marketing and sales professionals).

Benefits of using a toll-free service, either in-house or out-of-house, include the following:

- Applicants can easily apply without the need for a résumé.
- Candidates can call 24 hours a day, seven days per week, for optimum response rates.
- Applicants can get immediate feedback on the availability of open positions.
- It eases, and often eliminates, the paper burden of recruitment.
- An extensive applicant database can be created with the information collected at the time of the call for future use.
- This system can speed up the lead time for filling positions.

If your organization already has an 800 line installed for customers and vendors, it is quite easy to use this number for recruitment purposes. However, for small employers, for those on a limited budget without toll-free lines, and for those organizations with sporadic recruitment needs, the installation of a dedicated 800 number may not be practical.

Do not despair! Our capitalist society is a great thing, in that smart business owners have already seen this need, and are working with organizations to manage an 800 service for you. Often, these services are offered as part of a recruitment-advertising agency, or part of a telemarketing organization with skilled operators and staff to deal with responses in a proficient manner.

Typically, there is a minimum charge for using the service—usually around $500. Operators can be trained to merely complete an application

TABLE 5–1
Script for Toll-Free Service

Thank you for calling [name of company]. We'll ask you a few questions about your background that we will pass along to the recruitment manager. One of our recruitment managers will be calling you no later than [date].

1. What is the position title in the ad for which you are applying?
2. How many years of experience do you have in the position for which you are applying?
3. Who is your current employer?
4. What is your current position title?
5. What are your dates of employment with that employer?
6. Who is your previous employer?
7. How many years did you work for this employer?
8. Where did you see the advertisement for this position?

Thank you very much for calling [name of company].

---

form over the phone, or can even ask "knock out" or "disqualifying" questions. If you decide to ask these questions, ensure that the operators display the correct tone and manner when making these inquiries.

Organizations can elect to use a dedicated line, which costs more, or can have an extension in which the caller must correctly direct the call. Some systems permit a retrieval option, so that recruiters can download ad response from their database via modem.

These 800 features are generally offered in packages, depending upon the length of time that the ads are running, the volume of calls anticipated, and the specific services that are selected.

Table 5–1 demonstrates a questionnaire format used by one toll-free service. Of course, you can tailor questions to meet your specific needs.

In developing effective "800" advertisements, employers should ensure that the number is prominently displayed. For example, Wendy's International has used a graphic theme to reinforce the ease of calling. Their headlines, "The Answer Is At Your Fingertips . . . Dial Wendy's at 1-800- . . ." combined with a picture of the telephone entices candidates to call in if they feel "tired of doing the same thing day after day." In Figure 5–2, Red Lobster lures burned-out candidates to "Take Two Aspirins & Call Us In The Morning," followed with the toll-free number.

Restaurant Management

Take Two Aspirins & Call Us In The Morning
1-800-521-0249

Finding a better career opportunity doesn't have to be a painful experience. It's as easy as dialing our number and finding out why Red Lobster is #1.

Call Monday and ask us about:

— The stability and growth that leadership creates

— The impact of our expansion on your personal growth

— Our reputation for top quality in product and employee development

— The unique features of our compensation and bonus plan, including company paid relocation

Discovering a better alternative can be quite comforting.

Give us a call after 9AM this Monday, April 9th.

If unable to call, please send a resume outlining your management experience to: D. Kendrick, Red Lobster, Dept. NS48, 106 D East Marlton Pike, Cherry Hill, NJ 08034. Equal Opportunity Employer M/F.

Red Lobster®

FOR THE SEAFOOD LOVER IN YOU

Source: Courtesy General Mills Restaurants, Inc. and Bentley, Barnes & Lynn Advertising, Inc.

IDEA NO. 57: FORMALIZE WORD-OF-MOUTH ADVERTISING INTO TESTIMONIALS

There is no doubt about it; word of mouth continues to be one of the best forms of advertising. And one of the ways to use the benefits of this word-of-mouth advertising is through the use of testimonials in recruitment ads.

Testimonials are excellent for targeting specific labor-market segments, because they tell the prospective job candidate "I am just like you, I came to work for this company, and I am happy I did." This form of advertising is most effective when the copy and graphics of the ad work together to show the candidate that the happy employee is "just like them." You can use testimonials for women, minority groups, youth, older workers, persons with disabilities, and other labor-market segments. They may also speak to customers, career shifters, moonlighters, exiting military, and other target markets.

Testimonials can use photographs of actual employees or can feature models who are hired for the purposes of recruitment advertising. There are benefits on both sides of the equation: the ad gains credibility when an employee is used, especially when job candidates may know the employee personally; the advertisement becomes awkward if the employee leaves—especially under unhappy circumstances. When real employees are used, it is recommended that you obtain releases authorizing the use of their pictures in advertisements. Obtain legal counsel on the appropriate terminology for these releases.

Carefully select models to be used in recruitment ads. Observe style of dress and uniform, hair styles, and other "signals" to readers. For example, one employer made a terrible mistake in selecting models for an ad that was intended to target older workers. The company wanted to ensure that job candidates understood that they were interested in targeting older workers, so they selected models who had all the visible signs of being quite old. After doing some research, the company discovered that older individuals tended to identify themselves with pictures of people who were 7 to 15 years younger than they were. So, when a model was selected that looked to be at least 60 years of age, the company was then targeting workers who were 67 to 75 years of age and older. No wonder the company did not get much response!

Testimonials may also use caricatures, cartoons, or other artwork to depict employees. Carefully select artwork that is appropriate, given the nature and tone of the advertisement.

Walt Disney World in Orlando, Florida, has used a testimonial theme, depicting actual employees from a number of different departments, under the headline theme of "Disney Dream Maker." Each ad features a photograph of an employee with a short statement about why the employee likes working at Disney. The ads feature the positions of housekeeper and laundry worker and depict older and younger workers, minorities and non-minorities, and males and females.

Forest Hospital in Des Plaines, Illinois, also uses this approach to capitalize on word-of-mouth recruitment. Their ads feature quotes from a "Forest Staff RN" and the "Director of Nursing" without focusing on an individual or naming names. Yet the ads are most effective in that they tell the nurse, from a nurse's perspective, why their environment is a great place to be.

IDEA NO. 58: CAPITALIZE ON WRITE-IN ADS

In running a business, no one would consider making it difficult for the customer to buy the product or service. Yet many businesses place barriers for job candidates to overcome in deciding to work for a company.

Job candidates of yesterday were like customers shopping for a refrigerator when theirs had already broken down, says Paul Austermuehle, vice president of recruitment for Bentley, Barnes & Lynn, Inc., a recruitment-advertising agency in Chicago. "These candidates had a need, and they proceeded very directly to meet their needs," he explains.

The difference today is that candidates are just window shopping with nothing in mind, says Austermuehle. This changes the approach that employers must take.

A better approach must be similar to the approach taken for the "elusive" customer. The objective is not how to get the candidate to "buy"— to accept a position—but rather, how to move the candidate to learn more about the employment opportunity.

One way to permit candidates to explore the opportunity is to permit them to write or call in for more information. In the example shown in Figure 5–3, Walbro Corporation in Cass City, Michigan, is not requesting that candidates set up an interview right away, but is allowing the potential prospect to write in for more information or to have the company call to discuss various aspects of employment at Walbro.

FIGURE 5–3
Offer Candidates New Ways to Respond to Advertising

IMPATIENCE IS A VIRTUE
AT WALBRO

At Walbro Corporation, we have our own way of looking at things. And people. What some companies might call impatient, we think of as eager. And those are exactly the kind of people we're looking for.

Walbro is the $70 million designer of fuel system components for the automotive and small-engine industries. Our engineers and designers take pride in meeting new challenges and accepting new responsibilities. And we've got plenty for everyone — including you.

PROJECT ENGINEERS
Will design, develop, and test a variety of fuel systems components. A BSME and 3 or more years experience required.

DESIGNERS
Will design new products and improvements for existing products. An Associate's degree in Mechanical Design and 1 or more years experience required.

If you won't wait for responsibility, you want Walbro. Take on the assignments you deserve. You'll also receive a competitive salary and full benefit package. To find out more, send a resume with salary history, in strict confidence, to: Walbro Corporation, Attn: Salaried Employment, 6242 Garfield Ave., Cass City, MI 48726. An Equal Opportunity Employer M/F.

IN MICHIGAN, IT'S THUMBS UP FOR FUN AND FAMILIES! Michigan's "Thumb" offers a lifestyle that's hard to beat. The rolling fields and miles of lakeshore make it a four-season center for outdoor fun. The quiet streets, affordable housing, and exceptional educa-

tional facilities make it a paradise for families. And it's all within easy driving distance of Detroit, Flint, and Saginaw. For fun and for families, it's "thumbs up" in Michigan.

I CAN'T WAIT TO FIND OUT MORE ABOUT WALBRO!
_____ Rush me more information.
_____ Call me at home after _____ AM/PM.
_____ My resume is attached.
NAME _____
ADDRESS _____
PHONE _____
PRESENT EMPLOYER _____
POSITION _____ YEARS ____

WALBRO

Home of the
 Engineer

Source: Courtesy Walbro Corporation and Bentley, Barnes & Lynn Advertising, Inc.

Handy Andy, based in Schaumburg, Illinois, also offers a ''FREE BROCHURE'' to individuals interested in finding out more about their assistant manager and manager positions. Handy Andy even permits candidates a number of options as to how individuals might explore the opportunities: through the brochure, through an interview at an upcoming hardware show, or by sending a résumé. This company wants to give its candidates a number of options—making it easier on that elusive shopper.

IDEA NO. 59: CREATE POWERFUL HEADLINES TO ATTRACT ATTENTION

When your ad is competing with hundreds of other advertisements and messages for the attention of that reader, your ad must grab that reader. One powerful method to attract the reader is to use powerful headlines that convey your message and that beg the reader to read on!

Headlines can be fun, mysterious, humorous, serious, dramatic, or enticing. Just examine some of these headlines being used effectively by some successful employers today:

- ''Wanted: RNs with Attitudes'' and ''Wanted: RNs Who Talk Back''—Edgewater Medical Center, Chicago, Illinois.
- ''Toothpaste, Aspirin, Soda Pop, and $5 Billion''—Walgreen Co., Deerfield, Illinois.
- ''The Dough Is Rising''—ad for culinary specialists, Walt Disney World, Orlando, Florida.
- ''60 WPM and Aerobic Shoes Required''—ad for secretaries, Household Financial Services, Prospect Heights, Illinois.
- ''Aids. Cancer. Heart Disease. In 1988, We'll Put $400 million behind Your Efforts to Fight Them''—Abbot Laboratories, Abbott Park, Illinois.
- ''You didn't get your MBA just to be an MIA''—General Mills Restaurants, Austin, Texas.
- ''One, Two, Velcro My Shoe; Three, Four, Manage Our Store''—McKids Stores, Chicago, Illinois.

Some headlines work particularly well when combined with graphics. In Figures 5–4 and 5–5 Kraft General Foods uses the popular brand names that are so familiar to consumers and capitalizes on this with their headlines to attract systems professionals: "We've Got Billions of Ways to Perk Up Your Career" (Maxwell House), and "We're Stirring Up Technology, And We Want You In The Mix" (Kool-Aid).

The United Airlines ad shown in Figure 5-6 used a dramatic statement, "Let the Games Begin" and combined that message with simple, bold graphics of the Olympic torch. The Holiday Corporation advertisement in Figure 5-7 again combines the familiar corporate logos of Holiday Inn, Embassy Suites, Hampton Inn, and Harrah's, with the headline, "Who Else Could Invite The Entire City of Seattle To Stay Overnight?"

IDEA NO. 60: USE WHITE SPACE EFFECTIVELY

In this day of rising recruitment costs, all of us want to spend our recruitment dollars wisely. In fact, many managers responsible for placing ads have traditionally tried to pack in the most ad copy in the least amount of space in attempts to spend money most effectively. However, cramming lots of ad copy into a small amount of space may not be the best way of maximizing recruitment dollars, especially when examining the effectiveness of the recruitment ad.

Many copy-intensive ads get lost on a page of advertising—there is nothing to make the ad stand out on the page. One way to make an advertisement catch the attention of the reader is to make effective use of white space. Yes, it does cost money, but there are ways of using white space to gain valuable paybacks in terms of response rates.

Advertisements for secretaries are often lost in the classified section of the paper, crammed with copy, and lacking pizzazz to attract the reader's eye. Motorola, Inc. decided to change that approach and used enormous amounts of white space to make their ad stand out.

Red Lobster uses white space instead of graphics to make their point that they offer their employees room to grow (Figure 5-8).

Amoco Corporation mandates that graduates "Think BIG" in their ad that maximizes white space (Figure 5-9).

FIGURE 5–4

Combine Headlines and Graphics to Attract Attention

We've Got Billions Of Ways To Perk Up Your Career.

For Information Systems professionals, the $22 billion Kraft General Foods provides an open forum for state-of-the-art challenges and discovery. That's why we seek only the most professional business systems analysts.

We've taken on a systems development initiative that will change the way we do business throughout the world. Our current needs are:

PRODUCTION & DISTRIBUTION SYSTEMS
—Lead projects involving inventory control, MRP, warehousing and transportation
—Requires 2 years systems development experience with S/38 or AS 400

DATABASE ADMINISTRATION
—Evaluation, maintenance and supportive database systems
—At least 2 years of DB2, AS 400, Teradata or Ingres required

DATA SECURITY
—Design/implement security systems and enhancements
—Recommend corporate wide data security safeguards
—Requires at least 2-4 years of systems/business analysis experience with 2-4 years ACF2 experience

ORDER MANAGEMENT— SR. BUSINESS CONSULTANTS
—Plan, design and develop order management systems
—Requires MBA with 4-10 years experience in business systems/order processing systems

DECISION SUPPORT SYSTEMS— SR. BUSINESS CONSULTANTS
—Requires BS or MBA with 4-8 years related experience
—Knowledge of PCs, METAPHOR, SYSTEM W essential
—LANs (Ethernet or Token Ring) required

INSTALLED BASE SYSTEMS
—Requires strong analytical skills with background in systems development and testing
—At least 1-3 years of COBOL experience required

HUMAN RESOURCE INFORMATION SYSTEMS
—Design/develop Human Resource/Payroll systems
—At least 3-5 years mainframe development experience
—McCormack and Dodge or MSA a definite plus

Additional positions are available for:

—E-MAIL SOFTWARE PACKAGE DEVELOPERS
—TECHNICAL TRAINING MANAGERS
—END USER TRAINING MANAGERS

See us at our Suite. If unable to stop by, call 708/998-2125 or write to: C. Kucharyszyn, Systems, Kraft General Foods, Inc., Kraft Court, 4N, Glenview, IL 60025. Equal Opportunity/Affirmative Action Employer.

KRAFT GENERAL FOODS
A new brand of business.

Source: Courtesy Kraft General Foods and Bentley, Barnes & Lynn Advertising, Inc.

FIGURE 5–5
Capitalize on Your Corporation's Strong Image

We're Stirring Up Technology, And We Want You In The Mix.

IS DEVELOPMENT CENTER
IMPLEMENTING CASE TOOLS

Once again, $23 billion Kraft General Foods is taking the initiative with plans to create a leading edge IS development environment. As we bring IEW and other CASE Tools to Kraft General Foods for the first time, we seek the right team to implement it.

To join our state-of-the-art environment, we require IEW or other CASE Tool application experience. Microfocus COBOL a plus. Strong analysis experience required with a background in PCs.

Make a significant contribution to the way we do business around the world. Our commitment to IS development means you'll find an open forum for challenge and discovery. We provide an exceptional salary along with flex hours, a fitness center and a superb benefits package.

Find out more by sending a resume including salary history to: Kraft General Foods, Kraft Court, 4N-Beth Levine, Glenview, IL 60025. Equal Opportunity Employer M/F/H/V.

KRAFT GENERAL FOODS
A new brand of business.

Source: Courtesy Kraft General Foods and Bentley, Barnes & Lynn Advertising, Inc.

FIGURE 5-6
Combine a Dramatic Headline with Simple, Bold Graphics

LET
THE GAMES
BEGIN.

No four words in any language pack more power than these. They are words that competitors thrill to all over the world. They stand for something that is at the root of human endeavor.

At United Airlines competition is more than a game. It's a way of life for more than 60,000 men and women who are striving to be their best day in and day out.

We can't all be athletes. We can't all compete merely for the sake of competition. But we can derive the satisfaction of putting our entire effort against the highest standards.

Accountants. Financial Analysts. Computer Programmers. Engineers. Marketers. Sales Representatives. No matter what career path you walk, there is room for you in "the friendly skies."

Because here, the challenge doesn't end when they put out the torch.

Find out more about career opportunities with the world's greatest airline. Write in confidence to: Professional Employment. EXOPX—NUL, United Airlines. P.O. Box 66100, Chicago, IL 60666. Equal Opportunity Employer.

Source: Courtesy United Airlines and Bentley, Barnes & Lynn Advertising, Inc.

FIGURE 5–7
Use Corporate Logos to Increase Response Rates

Source: Courtesy Holiday Corporation and Bentley, Barnes & Lynn Advertising, Inc.

FIGURE 5-8
Use White Space to Attract Attention on the Page

Restaurant Management

Room to grow.

Are you starting to feel like you're part of a crowd? Are you wondering when your day will come? Maybe you should talk with the nation's most successful restaurant company—Red Lobster.

For the third straight year, Red Lobster leads the industry in number of units, market share and systemwide sales.

It's no wonder when you consider our 20 year tradition of quality. In product. In service. And in management. Of course it's not hard to attract the best management talent in the business when you can offer what Red Lobster can.

Where else can a manager enjoy a guaranteed five day work week. Quarterly bonuses. And, with 72 new Red Lobster restaurants in 24 months, outstanding career potential.

All we ask is that you bring us a winning attitude, leadership qualities and progressive management experience.

We're profitable. We're dynamic. We're growing. That means we can offer you room, with a view. For consideration, send your resume to: Al Spagnuolo, Red Lobster, Dept. HC56, 500 Grapevine Highway, Suite 224, Hurst, TX 76054. Equal Opportunity Employer.

FOR THE SEAFOOD LOVER IN YOU   **Red Lobster.**

Source: Courtesy General Mills Restaurants, Inc. and Bentley, Barnes & Lynn Advertising, Inc.

FIGURE 5–9
Combine White Space with Graphics to Increase Reader's Response

One thing most graduates have in common is an ability to think big. You're just starting out on your career. You've got great expectations, and great potential. Which is why it makes sense to give your talent the room it needs to grow. You'll find the room at Amoco. Amoco is a global energy and chemical enterprise with the resources to back up big ideas. At Amoco, you can do more than make a good living. You can make a big difference. And isn't that what a meaningful career is all about?

Amoco Corporation

Source: Courtesy Amoco Corporation and Bentley, Barnes & Lynn Advertising, Inc.

IDEA NO. 61: COLOR YOUR ADS

Cost-conscious managers want to reduce recruitment costs—but sometimes it pays to spend a little to gain big rewards. Using color is one way to enhance visibility on the page and to upscale the look of the advertisement.

Herman Miller, Inc., a designer and manufacturer of contemporary office furniture and office systems based in Zeeland, Michigan, uses color to attract the eye of the engineer. The ad in Figure 5–10 uses four-color in the photographs of the chairs to demonstrate an upscale image, and to tie in the theme of their product and the theme of the headline, "We Have a Few Seats Available for Engineers." Their ad in Figure 5–11 uses color in a simple, yet dramatic way, by combining the effects of white space in the segments "From Start . . ." and "To Finish" with the use of color in the words of the company—Herman Miller.

IDEA NO. 62: ADD UNUSUAL GRAPHICS
FOR IMPACT

Graphics are powerful tools of the recruitment advertiser. They send messages before the reader has even scanned the first words of the ad. They send subtle signals that draw that elusive shopper—the person who is not actively seeking an employment change—into stopping and considering the possibilities of such a change.

Like headlines, graphics can send a variety of messages, depending upon the motivation of the ad. Consider the following:

- Do you want to show that your work environment is a fun, enjoyable one?
- Do you want to overcome a stereotype?
- Do you want to position your organization in a new way?
- Do you merely want candidates to read your ad?
- Do you want to attract a new market segment?

Graphics can be effective in assisting the organization in realizing these goals.

FIGURE 5–10
Use Color to Create an Upscale Image

WE HAVE A
FEW SEATS AVAILABLE
FOR ENGINEERS.

If this were a typical recruitment ad, you could expect a litany of glowing adjectives to follow. A generous sprinkling of phrases like, ``a dynamic growth opportunity'' and ``good people make the difference'' would undoubtedly accompany the specific job descriptions.

And while we might be tempted to describe engineering opportunities at Herman Miller using similar language, we believe that people interested in working with us deserve a more candid picture of our company—which like-this ad, is anything but typical.

Should you come to work with us as an industrial engineer, a chemical engineer, or a mechanical engineer in manufacturing or product development, you'll find an environment every bit as innovative and open as the interior systems and furnishings we create. And, in return for your time, talent, and expertise, you will become a participative owner and be rewarded for your individual performance as well as for the overall performance of the company.

If you're intrigued by the notion of working with a company that thinks furniture is more than

materials, and that creativity is the product of individuals, not committees, then we'd like to talk with you.

Visit us at the NSBE Career Fair, Booth 230, on March 31. Or write to Staffing-M/S 7165, Herman Miller, Inc., 8500 Byron Road, Zeeland, MI 49464. An equal opportunity employer.

You'll come to know why we've been cited as one of The 100 Best Companies To Work For In America. And you'll find that while all our seats are comfortable, they are anything but typical.

⊔ herman miller

Source: Courtesy Herman Miller Inc. and Bentley, Barnes & Lynn Advertising, Inc.

FIGURE 5–11

Use of Color Is Dramatized When Coupled with White Space

Source: Courtesy Herman Miller, Inc. and Bentley, Barnes & Lynn Advertising, Inc.

113

IDEA NO. 63: CONTRAST YOUR ADS

One low-cost method to enhance the visibility of your ads is to make use of high contrast. Reversed copy—white lettering on a black background—is one of the easiest and least expensive methods of gaining high-contrast ads that jump out of a page of advertising.

IDEA NO. 64: EXPERIMENT WITH COUPON ADS

Since many of the candidates considered most desirable by employers are those who are currently working and without a prepared résumé, organizations benefit from finding ways to make it easy for the candidate to apply. Using clip-out coupons is one way to meet this need.

Employers can use clip-out coupons in almost any section of the newspaper. As mentioned, one employer, seeking women who might be reentering the workplace, placed coupon-type ads near the grocery store advertisements on coupon days. Organizations seeking secretaries with various word processing and computer skills are using coupon ads that permit interested candidates to merely check off the skills that they possess. Retailers and restaurants run coupon ads that encourage individuals to check the hours and days they are available for work. Even the Army National Guard has used clip-out coupons appearing in national publications.

Figure 5–12 demonstrates an advertisement by United Airlines for flight attendants fluent in Japanese!

IDEA NO. 65: CREATE A THEME FOR ADVERTISING

How do employers begin to build an image as a great place to work? One way that this can be accomplished is through the creation of a unified recruitment theme that ties together the various elements of a recruitment-advertising plan.

With advertising costs increasing all the time, employers must look for ways to gain impact with their limited budgets, and the creation of a re-

FIGURE 5–12
Use Clip-Out Coupons to Increase Reader Response

Source: Courtesy United Airlines and Bentley, Barnes & Lynn Advertising, Inc.

cruitment theme permits employers to accomplish this goal. Further, for employers with multiple locations regionally or nationally, there is an opportunity to maximize dollars through the use of a planned theme or campaign.

Figures 5–13 through 5–15 are excellent examples of how Rockford Memorial Hospital in Rockford, Illinois, used a unified theme to convey the announcement of their clinical ladder program for nurses. In using a theme of ''positive changes'' and ''change is progress'' they informed nurses in the community of this new addition at their hospital.

FIGURE 5–13
Create a Unified Advertising Theme

Positive Changes

Signing The Declaration Of Independence Gave The People New Power.

Our clinical ladder will do the same for your nursing career.

At Rockford Memorial Hospital, we're committed to the future of our nurses. And we've put action behind the words by implementing a new, nurse-designed Clinical Ladder.

Empowered with more control over the nursing process, our nurses now receive maximum recognition for their performance in a clinical role. Here are the elements:

• Self nomination for advancement, followed by nurse management and peer review.

• A 5-tier ladder with very clear-cut, well-defined distinctions between each level.

• Unique criteria for advancement: fulfillment of both qualifications and 'expectations,' which recognize nurses' selective and voluntary involvement in preferred areas.

• No waiting in line for promotion; no ceiling on growth.

At Rockford Memorial Hospital, we've made the changes that form the foundation for exciting careers. Find out your role in the clinical process at Rockford Memorial. Call Mary Beth Wallace to find out more about our clinical ladder and new salaries ranging from $22,000-$38,000/year. 815/961-6110, Rockford Memorial Hospital, 2400 N. Rockton Ave., Rockford, IL 61103. Equal Opportunity Employer.

●Rockford Memorial Hospital

Change Is Progress.

Source: Courtesy Rockford Memorial Hospital and Bentley, Barnes & Lynn Advertising, Inc. Photo supplied by Bettman Agency.

FIGURE 5–14
Recruitment Themes Stress the Benefits the Organization Is Selling to Prospective Job Candidates

Positive Changes

Their commitment to an idea changed our lives forever.

Our nursing clinical ladder can change yours.

At Rockford Memorial Hospital, commitment is not a word we take lightly. It underlies our belief in the nursing process— and in our nurses.

In collaboration with our nursing staff, we designed and implemented a Clinical Ladder that truly empowers nurses to attain their individual goals. Here's how:

• Self nomination for advancement, followed by nurse management and peer review.

• A 5-tier ladder with very clear-cut, well-defined distinctions between each level.

• Unique criteria for advancement: fulfillment of both qualifications and 'expectations,' which recognize nurses' selective and voluntary involvement in preferred areas.

• No waiting in line for promotion; no ceiling on growth.

Discover the new directions in store for you at Rockford Memorial Hospital. With our Clinical Ladder, your dreams are within reach. Call Mary Beth Wallace to find out more about our clinical ladder and new salaries ranging from $22,000-$38,000/ year. 815/961-6110, Rockford Memorial Hospital, 2400 N. Rockton Ave., Rockford, IL 61103. Equal Opportunity Employer.

Change is progress.

Source: Courtesy Rockford Memorial Hospital and Bentley, Barnes & Lynn Advertising, Inc.
Photo supplied by Bettman Agency.

FIGURE 5–15
A Unified Theme Helps to Reinforce the Message

Positive Changes

Along with the women's vote came new power.

Our nursing clinical ladder gives you new control over your future.

At Rockford Memorial Hospital, our nurses are empowered to achieve more than ever before. Because our new Clinical Ladder has given them a tremendous platform for recognition and advancement. And tremendous inspiration for the future.

We've collaborated with our nurses to design a career tool that directly addresses the issues of advancement in a clinical role. Here are the elements:

• Self nomination for advancement, followed by nurse management <u>and</u> peer review.

• A 5-tier ladder with very clear-cut, well-defined distinctions between each level.

• Unique criteria for advancement: fulfillment of both qualifications and 'expectations,' which recognize nurses' selective and voluntary involvement in preferred areas.

• No waiting in line for promotion; no ceiling on growth.

At Rockford Memorial Hospital, we've put a premium on making the changes that will keep your nursing career ahead of the rest. Maybe it's time to find out what your real strengths are. Call Mary Beth Wallace to find out more about our clinical ladder and new salaries ranging from $22,000-$38,000/year. 815/961-6110, Rockford Memorial Hospital, 2400 N. Rockton Ave., Rockford, IL 61103. Equal Opportunity Employer.

● RockfordMemorialHospital

Change Is Progress.

Source: Courtesy Rockford Memorial Hospital and Bentley, Barnes & Lynn Advertising, Inc. Photo supplied by Bettman Agency.

IDEA NO. 66: DEVELOPING POWERFUL ADVERTISING COPY

Advertising copy should be direct in its approach in order to encourage candidates to respond. While image advertising should be a part of any recruitment campaign, it is not what typically brings in the candidates to apply.

Other tips for strong ad copy includes the following:

- "You will" are the best words to use in recruitment advertising, much better than "you should" or "you will be expected to."
- Use the present tense.
- Use words proven to attract attention, such as *new* and *you*.
- Always show readers "what's in it for them."
- Use powerful words to attract attention, such as *opportunity*, *excellent salary package*, *exciting*, *management*.
- Avoid phrases such as "salary negotiable" and "applications invited," as these sound too desperate for a warm body.
- Write from a "you" point of view.

Consider individual advertisements and plural advertisements—those ads offering multiple positions. Individual ads will tend to be focused in their approach and will tend to attract only those candidates whose backgrounds most closely match the requirements for the position. Plural advertisements, since they offer many opportunities, will attract even those candidates whose backgrounds do not match the posted requirements, in hopes that other individuals may be needed. Use each approach appropriately, depending on whether you wish to gain a larger, less focused response versus a smaller, more focused response.

Sometimes recruiters do need to reduce the response, and in those cases, these qualifiers will help:

- "If you have. . . ."
- "Some . . . preferred."
- "Must have. . . ."
- "No beginners, please."
- "Minimum of. . . ."
- ". . . Helpful."

- "Background checks will be conducted."
- Blind advertising (responses sent to a post office box).[1]

Testimonials and endorsements make excellent ad copy. This can be a statement from a current employee or a typical statement that could be made about your organization.

Use graphics to link the visual message with the written word. Use symbols to dramatize the effect.

One final word about ad copy: make it easy to read. Use bullets to highlight key words and phrases. Break up copy as much as possible so that the eye can quickly scan your message. Choose readable type, such as a serif typeface such as Times Roman or Century Schoolbook, and select a type size large enough for the reader to quickly scan. Stay away from all uppercase type—all capitals—as these are more difficult to read.[2]

SUMMARY

Newspapers can be effective in today's difficult labor markets, but must be updated in order to attract the quality and quantity of candidates needed to meet staffing goals. Newspaper ads should be eye-catching, capturing the interest of the reader who is not actively seeking a new job. Advertisements should also be in places that are read by the nonjob seeker—in alternate sections of the paper and in alternate papers. Advertisements should make it easy for the candidate to respond and check out employment opportunities, through toll-free 800 numbers, through coupon ads, and with ads that permit the reader to gain further information.

By putting a new twist on an old theme, managers will find that newspaper advertising is still a viable opportunity for getting qualified candidates.

Ideas for Updated Approaches: The Newspaper

Idea No. 50: Using recruitment advertising agencies.

Idea No. 51: Look to other sections of the newspaper.

Idea No. 52: Use other newspapers.

Idea No. 53: Try display advertising.

Idea No. 54: Try classified ads!

Idea No. 55: Experimenting with blind advertising and the omission of corporate logos.

Idea No. 56: Installing or listing an 800 telephone number.

Idea No. 57: Formalize word-of-mouth advertising into testimonials.

Idea No. 58: Capitalize on write-in ads.

Idea No. 59: Create powerful headlines to attract attention.

Idea No. 60: Use white space effectively.

Idea No. 61: Color your ads.

Idea No. 62: Add unusual graphics for impact.

Idea No. 63: Contrast your ads.

Idea No. 64: Experiment with coupon ads.

Idea No. 65: Create a theme for advertising.

Idea No. 66: Developing powerful advertising copy.

Ideas for Updated Approaches: The Newspaper

Idea	Cost	Number People	Lead Time	Target
Idea No. 50: Ad agencies	L	—	S–L	Y
Idea No. 51: Other sections	M–H	—	S–L	Y
Idea No. 52: Other papers	L–H	—	S–L	Y
Idea No. 53: Display ads	M–H	—	S–M	Y
Idea No. 54: Classified ads	L–H	—	S	Y
Idea No. 55: Blind ads	L–M	—	S–L	N
Idea No. 56: An 800 number	L–H	M	M–L	N
Idea No. 57: Testimonials	L–H	M	S–L	Y
Idea No. 58: Write-in ads	L–H	—	S–L	Y
Idea No. 59: Powerful headlines	L–H	—	S–L	Y
Idea No. 60: White space	L–H	—	S–L	N
Idea No. 61: Color ads	M–H	—	M–L	N
Idea No. 62: Graphics	L–H	—	S–L	Y
Idea No. 63: Contrast ads	L–H	—	S–L	N
Idea No. 64: Coupon ads	L–H	—	S–L	N
Idea No. 65: Create a theme	L–H	M	S–L	Y
Idea No. 66: Powerful ad copy	L	—	S–L	Y

Key:

Cost		Lead time	
Low	0–$200	Short	0–1 week
Medium	$200–$1,000	Moderate	1 week–4 weeks
High	$1,000+	Long	4+ weeks

Number people		Target	
Single	1	Yes	
Multiple	2 or more	No	
Either			

ENDNOTES

1. Herschell Gordon Lewis, "Classified Is the Most Direct," *Direct Marketing*, September 1988, pp. 46–49.
2. Richard Siedlecki, "Small Ads, Big Response," *In Business*, May/June 1988, pp. 44–45.

Chapter Six

Developing and Implementing More Updated Approaches

A s with newspaper advertising, the "tried and true" methods to recruit must be changed, updated, and modified in order to attract the best and the brightest candidates—since many of these methods are not as effective as they should be to meet staffing goals. Therefore, strategies such as open houses, career and job fairs, school recruitment, and other more traditional forms of finding applicants must be changed and updated in order to attract the best.

IDEA NO. 67: HOLD AN OPEN HOUSE

What is an open house? Usually, an open house is a recruitment event, sponsored by one employer, held at the employer's place of business, or in a nearby hotel, community center, or other meeting place. Generally, it offers prospective employees the opportunity to check out job opportunities in a more informal, unstructured manner. This appeals to many candidates who may be unwilling to commit to a formal job interview, including labor-force reentrants or first-time entrants, or those who are fairly happy with their current employer but may want to see what else is "out there."

Open houses are an excellent strategy to consider when there are multiple openings to fill, since the cost is usually higher for this event. Also, since an open house can attract large numbers of applicants, it is also an opportunity to keep the cost-per-hire low.

In designing an open house, what are the primary considerations? One of the biggest dilemmas facing open-house planners is the question of how many people to expect. It can be a terrible experience if you plan for 30 people and 300 anxious applicants show up. There is no way you can handle the overflow. It is equally disastrous if you expect 300 people, rent a huge hall, enlist the help of large numbers of staff for the event, and only three candidates arrive. What's a recruiter to do?

One of the more ingenious ways recruiters can anticipate candidate flow is to hold a "call-in" open house, in which the open-house advertisement lists a number, and asks interested individuals to call in to schedule an appointment. This can boost participation rates in several ways. One is that many applicants may have questions about the job, the organization, or about their qualifications for the position. These are questions they would like to ask before giving up a free evening or weekend. The call-in number permits them to qualify themselves before making the commitment to attend.

Secondly, many open-house applicants, especially those who are currently working, may have doubts about attending an open house when an informant—perhaps someone from their current employer, or a friend of their current employer—may see them attending. By permitting interested people the opportunity to call you, you can reduce this risk by scheduling appointment times, hence enhancing participation rates.

Advertising for Open Houses

Participation rates for open houses are highly dependent upon the effectiveness of the advertising for the event. Mediums can include newspaper, magazine, television, radio, and direct mail. The method chosen depends upon the target audience and the positions being recruited. Often, recruiters are finding that a multimedia approach can often be best. For example, one recruiter found that by combining radio advertising that referred listeners to the newspaper ad, which included details about the open-house event, was an effective method for spreading the word.

When the target audience can be identified through a mailing list (see direct mail for more information), recruiters may advertise open houses by using this intrusive medium. One company chose to design their direct mailers to look like formal party invitations and found that response rates were high because of this unique and appealing approach.

Several organizations looking to fill multiple positions have found success in advertising on television for open-house events. LA County/USC

Medical Center used 30-second slots to convey a message about employment opportunities and tell about the biannual open houses being conducted.

The LA County/USC Medical Center approach was to feature an actor, posing as "Helen"—a fictional character based upon medical situations that occur within the hospital—an older woman with diabetes, complicated by an abusive home situation. As the viewer watches Helen sitting in a hospital ward, a narrator's voice says, "There was nowhere else to go, no one else to help her. Just us. This is the real-life drama of nursing." The ad ends with a close-up of Helen, while the narrator says, "If you're a registered nurse, come to our open house October 15. Helen needs you."

The television ad mirrored print-advertising campaigns, which featured six medical situations, taken from examples suggested by the nursing staff. The theme was designed to show the unique challenges of nursing within this hospital environment and to entice the kinds of nurses who found this work appealing and rewarding.

LA County/USC Medical Center was extremely pleased with the advertising campaign in that it raised awareness in the community about the work of the hospital, increased participation rates for the open house, and even enhanced retention by permitting the current nursing staff to play a role in the design and implementation of the commercial (real nurses were used as extras).

The cost for television is not inexpensive. Production costs were $22,500, plus the cost of placing the ads was $50,000 (the spots ran 20 times each on local and network stations for the spring and fall open houses).[1]

Walt Disney World near Orlando, Florida, also used television to publicize an open-house event that drew over 6,000 people, and resulted in hires for the 500 open positions.

The television campaign was one part of a multimedia blitz that included radio, newspaper, and point-of-sale messages. The advertising theme featured the familiar Mickey Mouse ears balloon, with narration that said, "You wouldn't be surprised if we told you we have one job available at Walt Disney World. Well, what might surprise you is that our plans for expansion mean more than 500 job opportunities throughout the Walt Disney World Resort. Seasonal, part-time and full-time. Right now. So don't be left out." Narration that followed included details for the two-day open-house event.

The cost for production was $13,600, with placement costs of $44,000.

Because of the success of the event, Disney ran a thank-you ad acknowledging the great turnout.[2]

Headlines for Attracting Open-House Participants

Whatever medium you select, use an appealing headline to attract participants to your open house. Consider these headlines used by companies:

- ''You've read about us, now meet the company behind the headlines.''—used by Abbott Laboratories to attract information systems professionals to their open house, capitalizing on Abbott's being named top company by *Computerworld* magazine.

- ''Back in 1776, it could take three days to reach our open house. Now it takes three days to have one.''—used by The New York Hospital/Cornell Medical Center to emphasize their longevity in the health care industry, inviting nurses to their three-day open-house event.

- ''Meet the international award-winning chefs of Walt Disney World.''—featured by Disney World in Lake Buena Vista, Florida, to attract culinary professionals to their one-day open house event in New Orleans, Louisiana.

- ''Something's up at Household Bank.''—run by Household Bank to attract candidates for customer service representatives, account managers, management trainees, loan processors, loan clerks and switchboard operators.

- ''Our open house will open some eyes Monday, March 13.''—featured by United Airlines to attract professionals in the MIS field.

- ''Come on out to our $22 billion spread'' (a graphic of Cheez Whiz was pictured).—used by Kraft General Foods for their MIS open house.

- ''We don't want you to just change jobs, change . . . your life/your lifestyle/your career potential/your income, responsibility, security . . .''—an open-house advertisement for restaurant management positions with Red Lobster.

- ''Dozens of brand new openings. Only one open house'' (pictured was a graphic illustration of cartoon chicks hatching).—an advertisement for management positions with Long John Silver's Seafood Shoppes.

Other Considerations for Open Houses

In orchestrating an effective open house, what are some of the elements to be considered?

1. **Should you conduct the open house within your own facility, or should it be held at a hotel, community center, or some other facility?** The overriding issue here is this—is your facility a selling point? If you have a state-of-the-art facility that is a selling point of employment, there can be a strong argument for holding the open house in-house. There are some other issues, however, including the convenience of the location, availability of free parking, the size of the facility (can it comfortably accommodate the numbers of people you are expecting?), and internal logistics.

    Should you decide to hold the open house away from your facility, consider these elements as well. One human resource professional was horrified when it was learned that the conveniently located hotel for the open-house event was right in the middle of major street repairs, with confusing detours. It was like a maze trying to find the hotel entrance, which may have been one of the reasons there were so few job candidates in attendance.

2. **How many people should you enlist to help staff the event?** When you're planning a call-in open house, you can more easily predict the number of applicants expected at any given time, or you can even limit the number of applicants for a specific time period. However, if you are planning a come-in open house, use your best judgment from previous events. Ideally, candidates should either be assisted by a staff person at all times, or else be occupied by a review of literature, completion of application forms, or review of video tapes. Calculate the time needed for a staff person to accompany each applicant, and staff accordingly.

3. **Who should staff the open house?** In addition to recruiters and human resource professionals, line managers and others involved in the hiring process should help staff the open house, depending upon the numbers of those needed to effectively meet and greet job candidates. Ideally, the staff at the open house should be representative of all labor-market segments, including women, men, minorities and nonminorities, to encourage candidates of these labor groups.

    Staff members, especially those who are not recruiters and familiar with the selling opportunities should be acclimated with how to positively position the features, advantages, and benefits of employment with the organization. Those responsible for the event may even provide staff with a ''cheat sheet'' of the selling features so that the staff can talk comfortably on these issues.

4. **Should you offer refreshments? Giveaways? Organization literature?** While the candidate is at the open house, there is a selling opportunity. Offer refreshments to make the applicant feel more welcomed. Inexpensive giveaways can be another fun way to help the candidate remember the open-house event, in addition to company literature. Tailor the giveaways to the target audience; for example, calculators might be given to business professionals, a software game could be given to MIS pros, and a cap or T-shirt could be given to entry-level candidates. Health care organizations have even provided watches with second hands to hard-to-recruit nurses.

5. **How will the open house flow?** Consider the manner in which candidates will be greeted, and how they will progress through the open house. For example, you may want a staff member to initially greet guests, acquaint them with the sequencing of open-house activities, and seat them for an introductory video. Then, perhaps, for an in-house open house, another staff member may take small groups or individuals on a tour of the facility. Applicants might then complete an application form before they are interviewed by a recruiter/interviewer. Finally, escort applicants to the door for farewells. Think through what it is you want to accomplish during the open house and the impression you wish to leave on the job candidates, and plan each detail meticulously.

IDEA NO. 68: TAKE AN OPEN HOUSE ON THE ROAD

When you are recruiting regionally or nationally for positions, why not take your open house on the road? Companies such as Houston-based Compaq Computer Corp. does just that in an effort to keep up with the strong growth of this computer company.

Compaq focuses their open-house events on one city at a time, with a multimedia approach. The open house is held in a major hotel in which Compaq creates a park-like environment with a 10-by-20 foot, four-color mural of the company's manufacturing headquarters. As many as 35 Compaq staff are on hand to manage the event.

Before each event, advertising takes the form of newspaper display ads, radio and television commercials, and direct-mail invitations.

When applicants show up at the event, they are registered and assigned a recruiter. Applicants get a chance to see the Compaq products, talk with systems engineers, review literature, and watch a video. Next, candidates have refreshments while they talk with recruiters in an informal interview session. Department managers then talk with candidates in a more formal 20- to 30-minute session before candidates are escorted to a relocation suite, with information on the Houston area.

The events draw about 1,000 candidates per event, with 1 out of 10 selected for next-step interviewing in Houston, with 4 to 5 hired. Compaq feels that the $100,000 investment per event is well spent, given the exceptional image awareness gained by this activity.[3]

Remote open houses don't have to be expensive to be effective. One employer, hoping to lure candidates to the central Florida market (with relatively low unemployment rates) went to Houston, Texas (with relatively high unemployment rates), to hold an open house. The company asked candidates to call in to schedule an interview, thus controlling the flow of candidates.

The company held the open house in a hotel, with suites for interviewing and hosting candidates. A local realtor was on hand to discuss selling of homes in the area; home and apartment listings were available in the suite regarding the Tampa and Orlando real estate markets.

Candidates received an introduction to the company, and could talk with real estate agents as they waited for an interview. The company scheduled in-depth interviews on the spot, so that they could make offers before the recruiters returned home. They made reference checks from the hotel and extended offer calls.

The open house was a success, with several management positions being filled with high-caliber candidates. The only additional expenses over and above a local open house were the travel expenses for the three recruiters.

IDEA NO. 69: PARTICIPATE IN A CAREER FAIR OR JOB FAIR

Job fairs and career fairs are growing in importance, says a survey conducted by Globe Research Corp. of *Recruitment Today* magazine subscribers. More than half—54 percent—of 568 respondents say their organizations participate in this recruitment event.[4]

The difference in open houses and career and job fairs is that open houses generally are sponsored by one employer, while career and job fairs are sponsored by multiple employers. The difference in a career fair and a job fair is generally the level of the positions being sought by employers. For example, professional and technical fairs are called career fairs, while job fairs are usually for entry-level and hourly positions.

Fairs can be sponsored by a third party, which administers all of the logistics for the fair, including the enlistment of participating employers and advertising for the event. Employers pay a fee to participate in the fair, with the fee based upon the level of the candidates being recruited.

Career and job fairs are also sponsored by high schools, colleges, vocational schools, government-funded employment and training programs, chambers of commerce, professional associations, and employer groups. You don't need to wait to be invited to participate in a career fair; initiate the event with other employers in your community. One retailer decided to orchestrate a job fair with other employers in the community and worked with the local mall as the site location. The fair was a huge success; however, the employers will no longer be permitted to hold their event at the mall: so many mall employees visited the fair and left their current employers that the mall businesses protested!

In planning a career or job fair, answer these questions to enhance the effectiveness of your efforts.

1. **Are you attending the right fair?** There are many types of fairs—and not all will be right for your organization. One fast-food recruiter attended a career fair held at one of the premier colleges for food-service management, only to find the majority of the students interested in careers with the prestigious hotel chains. The travel expense and the time to attend this fair was a waste of resources.

2. **What kinds of booths will be used by your competitors?** Many employers have purchased elaborate booths that are used throughout the year for a variety of recruitment purposes. Make sure that you have a competitive "look" with the other employers participating. There is nothing worse than attending a fair with a display poster, tablecloth, and a few handout materials, only to find that the competition has multimedia presentations, bright lights, expensive four-color brochures, and expensive giveaways. Do your homework so that you will feel confident and competitive.

You can purchase booths from companies that specialize in these products in the $500 to $2,000 price range. You can use these booths for multiple recruitment purposes and share them within your organization with marketing and public relations departments (including the costs!). Consider purchasing a booth that is easy to set up, store, ship, and carry.

3. **Who will be staffing your booth?** To be effective, you need to have your recruitment booth staffed with individuals who can sell candidates on the employment opportunities with your organization. Offer nonrecruiters a ''cheat sheet'' of ideas and benefits they should stress to job candidates. Suggest that they stand in front of the display as a means of removing barriers. They shouldn't be afraid to encourage job-fair attendees to come over to your table to discuss what you have to offer, and should approach the day with high energy. Apathetic, uninvolved people in your booth can do more harm than good to your recruitment efforts.

4. **What giveaways will be provided?** You may need something to encourage attendees to come to your booth—a small gift, prize, or even a drawing for a prize. A prize drawing can be very effective, because it not only gives you an opportunity to get more traffic at your booth, but it also permits you to capture the names, addresses, and phone numbers of the fair participants. You can use this mailing list to thank candidates for their time and encourage them to come and make a formal application with your organization, or, several months later, you can encourage applicants, who may now have found that their first employment choice is no longer an option, to come and reconsider employment opportunities with your organization. Follow-up activities can take the form of a direct-mail piece or telemarketing activities.

IDEA NO. 70: PLAN AN INFORMATION SEMINAR

An information seminar is similar to an open house in that it is sponsored by one employer in an attempt to recruit job candidates. It differs in one important respect, however. Where the advertised intent of the open house is to explore job opportunities with the employer, the advertised intent of the information seminar is to present some sort of information to the applicant, or prospective applicant.

Information seminars can be blatantly employment-oriented, or can project a more subtle appeal. Since many candidates may not be actively seeking employment, the information "carrot" can be another way to entice the candidate to explore the employment opportunity. One business, for example, found that only a handful of candidates would respond to an open-house event. But, when they conducted an information seminar on job-search skills at the same hotel, they experienced a full house. Of course, the information seminar ended with a commercial for the employer, and recruiters were standing by to conduct initial interviews. This employer found extraordinary success in attracting both quality and quantity of candidates using this value-added approach to the open house.

Other employers are using this approach to increase response rates. One such organization is Abbott Laboratories, sponsoring a summer internship presentation at the local university. Disney World has sponsored information sessions for their culinary apprenticeship programs, and Mercer Meidinger Hansen has held on-campus presentations preceding on-campus interview days.

TempWorld, a temporary help agency in Atlanta, Georgia, has teamed up with Rich's department stores to hold information seminars targeted at women who are considering a return to the work force. The seminars are free, by reservation only, and are held in special meeting rooms at the Rich's locations.

Advertising for the events take the form of in-store signs, ads in the Sunday newspaper, and radio spots. TempWorld has even appeared on local noontime talk shows to publicize the events. Each event costs about $5,000.

Local banks and chambers of commerce conduct similar information seminars twice each year in Birmingham, Alabama.[5]

IDEA NO. 71: USING EXECUTIVE-SEARCH FIRMS

Executive-search firms are third-party recruiting organizations, generally providing searches at the director, vice-president, president, and CEO levels. They are usually paid on a retainer basis, based upon 30 percent of the executive's base salary, and receive one third of the fee in advance, one third midway into the search, and the final third at the completion of the search. The firms often invoice expenses on a monthly or bimonthly basis.

The level of services offered by executive search firms is more extensive than those provided by recruitment agencies. Search firms often provide monthly status reports, with extensive background profiles for those candidates being considered, analysis of search status, and background and reference-check reports. Search firms will often give advice on search requirements, position titles, salary ranges, benefits and perquisites, and other search criteria.

When and why do organizations use the services of executive search firms? Consider these reasons:

- A smaller employer does not have the internal resources to conduct a high-level search and needs the input from professionals.
- The search is highly confidential—often because the incumbent is still in position—and a third party is needed to work to maintain this confidentiality.
- There is an extremely small population of qualified candidates that is difficult for the employer to appropriately identify for recruitment purposes.
- The cost of conducting an internal search is comparable to the cost for using a third party.

Before selecting an executive search firm, consider these issues:

- Do you like the people you'll be working with?
- Have you checked the search firm's references?
- Have you checked the references of the recruiter you'll be dealing with on the assignment?
- Who are the firm's clients?

Realize an executive-search firm will not recruit candidates from their current client base.

In managing the search assignment, recognize that an executive-level search is likely to take four to eight months to complete. Further, it is not uncommon for executives to give one month's notice before accepting the new assignment (and some prefer vacation time before jumping into the new environment). Anticipate human resources needs, and plan for the search as far in advance as possible.

IDEA NO. 72: WORKING WITH RECRUITMENT AGENCIES

Recruitment agencies are typically third-party recruiters that work with employers to place their job applicants. While executive-search firms place executive-level candidates, recruitment agencies can fill positions ranging from entry-level and hourly occupations to skilled, technical, professional, and managerial positions.

Recruitment agencies can receive payment in a number of ways. Some work on a retained-search basis; others receive payment from the employer only when they place an applicant. A few, particularly those working with hard-to-place candidates, may receive payment from the applicant.

Generally, agencies charge a standard rate of 1 percent per thousand dollars of base annualized salary, up to a maximum fee of 30 percent. Thus, an applicant who would be hired at an annualized base salary of $15,000 would have a fee of 15 percent, or $2,250; a base salary of $27,000 would have a corresponding fee of 27 percent, or $7,290; a base salary of $30,000 or more would have a fee of 30 percent, or $12,000 for a salary of $40,000, for example.

There are a number of new breeds of agencies and third-party resources cropping up today. These are discussed in Chapter Three in the section on new agencies.

In selecting a recruitment agency, carefully check references with other employers using their services. Make sure you are dealing with a reputable and ethical agency with a track record of professionalism. Unfortunately, there are still agencies who are unscrupulous in placing candidates, receiving their fees, and then working to place them with another competitive employer.

Also, work closely with the agency to determine what services they can provide, and match those with your needs. Make sure you are paying only for those services most needed, and negotiate with the agency if they are providing services you do not want or need.

Many agencies will work on a reduced-fee basis for a number of reasons:

- You choose not to take certain services, such as traditional 90-day guarantees that are often offered.

- You offer the agency an "exclusive"; in other words, you agree to work only with one agency on a search.

- You offer the agency multiple positions to fill.
- You provide the agency a limited exclusive, for example, for 30 to 90 days.
- You state that you will pay only a certain amount for a fee, and stick to your policy.

Just remember you are in the driver's seat in negotiating fees *before* you have seen a résumé or interviewed the candidate. Once you have shown interest to the agency, you greatly diminish your bargaining power. This is the reason many agencies send unsolicited résumés to employers—an attempt to "hook" the employer into doing business. For this reason, many employers have adopted the policy of discarding any unsolicited résumés from agencies—no exceptions. This also protects the employer when a candidate is hired who had been recruited directly by the company, but whose résumé was also sent unsolicited by the agency at the time of the employer's search.

In managing the agency relationship, work with your agency representative to set the guidelines for the search. You may elect to work with only one agency representative in order to provide effective lines of communications regarding feedback on candidates, the status of the search, and other related data.

Communicate often with your agency representatives, and let them know when they hit the mark, as well as when candidates do not match the job specifications. Be sure to work with the agency to let them know of your affirmative-action needs and goals.

IDEA NO. 73: DEVELOP COMPELLING RECRUITMENT BROCHURES AND LITERATURE

Recruitment brochures and literature have long been a staple for recruiters. They are the key marketing piece that lets candidates know the features, advantages, and benefits of employment with the organization. Since they also convey the culture and philosophy of the organization, they can be a powerful recruitment tool.

Here are some ideas in preparing your brochure for top effectiveness.

- **Is it versatile?** Does it need to be? If you traditionally recruit for a variety of positions, you may want to use a folder with optional pieces so that the materials can be tailored to the specific needs of the candidate and are appropriate to the position.

- **Does it sell candidates on what's in it for them?** Instead of developing a brochure that is a showpiece for the company, ask yourself, "Does this brochure let candidates know what we have to offer them—or is this just an attempt to puff up our ego and make us look good?"

- **Does it appeal to males and females, minorities and nonminorities, older workers and younger workers, disabled and nondisabled candidates?** If you include pictures or illustrations of employees, is the total gamut of work-force diversity represented? If not, you may be sending an inadvertent message to candidates that only white, male, younger, nondisabled candidates are being sought for employment.

- **Is there some easy way for candidates to respond to you?** Consider using a postage-paid business-reply card or coupon, or include a toll-free number for interested candidates to call *for more information*—it's important that you don't restrict candidates who aren't quite ready to proceed with the formal interview. Cole Vision Corporation uses a brochure with the postage-paid reply card, designed with a perforated edge so that it could easily be mailed. It also lists an 800 toll-free number to offer interested candidates alternatives for responding.

- **Consider how the brochure will be used.** For example, will its primary use be at high school job fairs, where you'll want to give out hundreds of brochures to entice youth to apply for entry-level summer jobs? If so, you may want to design a lower-cost brochure so that you can distribute it to all potential job candidates. Conversely, if the main use is for a smaller number of professional candidates, you might develop a high-profile brochure to project a strong employment image.

IDEA NO. 74: DEVELOP A VARIETY OF RECRUITMENT COLLATERAL MATERIALS—T-SHIRTS, BUMPER STICKERS, COFFEE MUGS, BUTTONS

Recruitment themes are popping up everywhere, including T-shirts, bumper stickers, coffee mugs, and buttons. Kentucky Fried Chicken developed a recruitment theme, "The place to be is KFC," and used the theme in display advertising as well as on T-shirts worn by employees and recruiters on specially designated work days and off days.

IDEA NO. 75: CREATE FORMAL AND INFORMAL EMPLOYEE-REFERRAL SYSTEMS

Employee referral is one of the most effective methods to attract qualified, loyal, hard-working employees. The cost per hire is generally lower, candidate quality is higher, and rate of attrition is lower. American Tool & Die saw a reduction in employee turnover from 27 percent to 4 percent by focusing on employee referrals and self-advertising.[6] One reason this is true is possibly because employees are interested in referring individuals who will work hard and carry their share of the work. Also, assuming that the employee wants to maintain a good reputation with their current employer, the employee is likely to recommend for employment those people who have similar standards for performance.

One drawback—or benefit—of employee referral is that it tends to replicate the makeup of the current work force. If your organization has a wide representation of minorities, women, older workers, and disabled workers, you are likely to replicate that mix. However, for employers lacking this desired diversity, employee referral may be a recruitment activity to be balanced with other activities.

Similarly, employee referral can be an excellent recruitment tool when current employees are qualified, hard-working employees. If, however, your current employee base leaves something to be desired, you may not want to use this recruitment strategy!

Many employers find that informal referral systems—those without incentives—can work effectively in certain environments. Two major principles of employee-referral systems should be followed for best results.

Principle one: Give it hype!   The general rule of employee referral is that when first initiated, employees will make referrals. After a period of time, however, interest wanes and referral rates diminish. To keep interest in the program going, you need to constantly remind employees of your interest in their referrals. Promote your need for referrals via payroll stuffers, posters, pep talks at staff meetings, and through other employee communication vehicles.

Principle two: Target new employees. As sad a comment as it may be on the employment picture, the happiest moment of employment with an organization may well be those first days on the job, when new employees are truly excited about the new job! Use this bit of information to your benefit in designing employee-referral systems. Talk about the referral program during the new-employee orientation, and encourage new employees to refer their former co-workers, along with their friends, neighbors, and other professional associates. Be more aggressive in your approach, and request that each new employee submit at least one name, address, and phone number for a referral. Then, take action yourself by contacting this referral directly about employment opportunities.

Other suggestions for designing formal incentive programs for employee referral include the following.

- **Award incentives that are appropriate for the level of the position, and that are attractive to employees.** Incentives can take the form of prizes, money, gift certificates, or points that can be exchanged for gifts. To determine the value of the incentives, many employers are computing their cost per hire (see Chapter Eight) and are offering something less than this amount for referrals. Ask your employees through an employee task force what they would like to receive as their incentive within this price range. Fidelity Systems in Boston designed a sweepstakes program and was able to fill 47 percent of some 150 open positions within a six-month period. The organization reduced its cost per hire by 50 percent, while seeing an increase in employee morale.[7]

- **Make the rewards as immediate as practical.** Some employers have retention rates tied in to referral programs. This just doesn't make sense, since the employee has very little control over the tenure of their referred friends. Increasingly, employers are making the payouts within a one-month period and eliminating multiple-payment schemes that have become administrative nightmares for recruiting staff. By making payments more immediate, they reinforce the desired behaviors, encouraging more referrals.

- **Change the program to keep interest high.** You can change various program elements to keep interest levels high. Experiment with changes in the awards or prizes, the time periods of operation, or with the positions for which incentives are given.

- **Use employee referral only during peak-need periods.** Many employers are eliminating ongoing programs, unless their recruitment needs are truly ongoing in nature. Organizations with peak staffing needs are finding that employee referral works well when only used for a specific period of time. Some retailers, for example, are discovering that a pre–Christmas season referral program is a great way to meet their staffing needs for this time period. Other employers are introducing a new prize or award during these peak needs to encourage more participation. One employer, for example, offers a special prize drawing during months with high recruitment needs: everyone who refers someone who is hired during this period receives, in addition to the regular award, a chance for a special prize drawing.

- **Keep the administrative process as simple as possible.** When there is any question as to whether or not an employee qualifies for an incentive, decide in favor of the employee. It just doesn't pay to quibble over who gets the credit for the referral—it only serves to lower morale and response rates.

Sometimes employee referral may work a little bit too well. Case in point: one company found that a particular employee tended to have an incredible record of referring friends. One day, the human resource manager asked the newly referred employee about his friend who had referred him. The new employee replied that he had never heard of this employee before being recruited by him. Upon further investigation, the organization learned that the employee with the incredible record for referral had been placing classified ads, at his own expense, in a variety of papers, making the referrals, and gaining the bonuses from his efforts. This company discovered that they could learn a lot from this innovative employee!

IDEA NO. 76: TAP INTO GOVERNMENT-FUNDED EMPLOYMENT AND TRAINING PROGRAMS

There are numerous government-funded employment and training programs available to assist employers in finding and training candidates for open positions. Many of these programs offer incentives to employers to hire their program participants, in the form of tax credits, reimbursements, and extensive, tailored training. Here are some suggestions for making the best use of the local services available in your area.

1. **Take the first step, and identify the programs with services available in your community.** One excellent resource is your Private Industry Council (PIC), which administers Job Training Partnership Act (JTPA) funds. Ask for a listing of the names, addresses, and telephone numbers of the subcontractors providing services within your area. This listing may change on a yearly basis, so be sure that you have the most recent listing.

2. **Make an appointment, and meet the program directors and counselors for these programs.** Find out more about the specific services and incentives that may be offered. Also, take the opportunity to introduce your organization and to investigate ways in which you can work together. Be prepared to sell the opportunities of employment with your company.

3. **Work to provide two-way communications with the program.** Find out how you can work more effectively, and provide good feedback on the candidates being referred.

4. **Consider an "on-campus" day in which you invite program directors and counselors to visit your organization.** Provide a tour to give the program staff a feel for the daily operations of your business, and design some presentations from managers and employees to talk about why your organization has a lot to offer.

5. **Investigate how you can benefit from Targeted Jobs Tax Credit (TJTC) and other incentives.** Contact your PIC or Department for Employment Services for more information.[8]

IDEA NO. 77: ON-CAMPUS RECRUITMENT, OTHER COLLEGE RECRUITING IDEAS, AND SCHOOL-RECRUITMENT IDEAS

Whether you are recruiting at a college, vocational school, or high school, the first step is to analyze the school to determine if this is a wise place to spend time and money. Too many times, organizations get caught up in recruiting at the college or high school where the recruiter attended (or worse yet, where the CEO graduated!). Many recruiters are beginning to find that when their efforts are diluted by too many assignments, they don't end up attracting the best and the brightest students. A better strategy is to concentrate efforts on one or two schools (more if your company is fortunate enough to have staff dedicated strictly to college recruitment) that can meet your staffing goals.

What criteria should be used in selecting the schools for focused recruitment efforts? Consider the following:

1. Is the curriculum offered a match with the job skills and abilities needed by your organization?

2. What is the demographic mix of students by sex, race, age, and other characteristics? Will this school be able to contribute toward your meeting affirmative-action goals? One human resource professional notes that a community college in her area tended to have a slightly older student population, where many of the students were already working and either putting themselves through college or benefiting from their employers' tuition programs. She found that these students tended to be more mature, had a more realistic picture of the world of work, and tended to make better performers with longer job tenure.

3. Will the school size provide you with enough students to meet your staffing needs?

4. Does the school location make sense? Further, do graduates of this school tend to stay in the communities in which you have business operations? Or do these students tend to move and settle in other locations?

5. What placement services are provided? Is it easy to work with the placement staff? Are department heads and professors accessible?

6. What are your past successes from this school? Even though it can take a while to establish a reputation on campus, is it worth it? Do you have the time, money, and other resources to maintain the momentum and develop some successes?

7. Who is your competition? Give up on those schools where the graduates are uninterested in careers in your industry or in your organization.[9]

Once you have made the decision as to what schools will be best for your recruitment efforts, the next step is to put together the program elements for your campaign. Undoubtedly, the most effective school-recruitment programs are those that involve the development of relationships with the school staff—counselors, teachers and professors, department heads, and program directors. Consider these elements for a school recruitment program:

- Serve on school advisory boards.
- Make contributions to the school in time, money, or equipment.
- Become involved in school-placement associations, such as the College Placement Council.
- Sponsor events, such as open houses, career and job fairs.
- Participate in career and job fairs sponsored by the school.
- Give presentations to classes, clubs, and student groups on job-search skills, careers within your industry, and other related topics.
- Teach a class.
- Schedule on-campus interviewing.
- Invite students to visit your organization.
- Provide internships for teachers and professors interested in broadening their horizons.
- Develop internships and cooperative study programs for students.[10]

While internships can be an excellent method to attract students, don't fall into the trap that one employer discovered. Supervisors at this company were ecstatic that they finally had much-needed help in the form of their summer interns, and decided to "dump" all of the unwanted tasks on these unsuspecting souls. While the supervisors met their short-term goals by getting the work done, and even improved morale by alleviating some of those unsavory duties, the internship did not achieve its goal of enticing these college students to consider employment with this organization. In fact, the opposite occurred, and the students had such a bad taste about their employment experience that they not only didn't consider further employment opportunities there, but they also told their fellow students about their terrible work experience.

A New Approach to College Recruitment

Since the name of the game in college recruitment is to create the right image and reputation in the minds of students at an increasingly earlier time (and not waiting until the time of graduation—too late—they've already made up their minds!), employers are looking for new methods to create this image. One service being offered by First Focus Publishers is the development and publication of a custom newsletter, mailed to college students majoring in computer disciplines. First Focus works with the client company to develop the articles, publish the newsletter, and direct-mail the recruitment piece to targeted students. Advanced Systems Applications is one company that has used the newsletter approach, calling their publication "Career Survival News." The publication helped students learn about and prepare for challenging careers in data processing, while positioning their organization as a leader in the industry.

First Focus Publishers also publishes *Field Guide to Computer Careers*, in which employers can purchase advertising space. The publication is distributed to students majoring in computer disciplines in colleges across the country.

IDEA NO. 78: USING TRADE PUBLICATIONS AND POPULAR MAGAZINES FOR RECRUITMENT MESSAGES

You can see recruitment ads and messages in almost every kind of publication—from trade publications and professional journals to popular magazines. In most trade and professional magazines, you can place classified or display-type advertising announcing your position opening. Check with your local library for a listing of these publications, or call one of the national professional or trade associations that can advise you of these journals.

Some companies are finding that stories about their organizations can be one way to create the image of a strong employer. Write to or call the publication editor to get an idea of what kinds of information are wanted, how articles are to be submitted, and other guidelines for publication. Provide press releases to magazines to let them know of activities taking place that may be of interest.

American Airlines has discovered an ideal magazine for placing advertisements for recruitment purposes—their own in-flight publication—*American Way*. Their first attempt was an ad seeking flight attendants, with the slogan, "At 35,000 feet—our flight attendants are down to earth." The ad drew 3,000 requests for applications. In their second attempt, they sought flight attendants fluent in foreign languages. This ad featured foreign phrases, which said, "We speak German, French, Spanish, and Japanese," then asked, "Do you?" Fifteen hundred requests for applications were received.

One of the intriguing elements of American's ad campaign was that the magazine advertising was read by frequent travelers, who actually spread the word about the opportunities to nonreaders of the publication. Actual candidates were the pass-along market.[11]

IDEA NO. 79: NETWORKING AND RECRUITING THROUGH TRADE AND PROFESSIONAL ASSOCIATIONS

Word of mouth is still one of the best forms of advertising, and so it is with recruiting as well. Recruiters should get the word out with friends in the community about position openings. By being a local chapter member of the Society for Human Resource Management or other professional associations, human resource professionals can network to discover strategies, methods, and activities that might be helpful in sourcing qualified candidates.

Another method for networking is through contacting the professional or trade association representing the position for which you are recruiting. For example, by calling the local or state chapter of the Society of Certified Public Accountants you can access a number of different placement services offered to members. While the level and variety of services offered range from organization to organization, inquire about these services provided:

- Résumé services.
- Membership database access.
- Classified advertising in newsletters and magazines.
- Membership rosters.
- Placement services offered at conferences.

IDEA NO. 80: MANUAL AND COMPUTERIZED IN-HOUSE POSTING SYSTEMS

Posting job openings on in-house bulletin boards is a traditional form of internal recruitment still being used by a large percentage of employers today. According to a survey conducted by Talent Tree Personnel Services, 45 percent of those responding to the survey still use this traditional recruitment activity. According to the vice president of training and development for the organization, "Companies are working harder than ever to retain their most valuable resource: the employee," and find that in-house posting programs permit accessibility to advancement opportunities within the organization. Twelve percent of companies who don't use the bulletin board *do* post job openings in company newsletters.[12]

One company that is taking job posting from the traditional to the non-traditional is National Semiconductor in Santa Clara, California. Employees can use terminals at their desks, or call from home using a terminal or personal computer (PC) and modem 24 hours a day, seven days per week. Employees can inquire regarding specific positions and eligibility requirements, as well as career-path information and gaps in education and experience for attaining the next step in the ladder.

Employees can also take action via the computer, entering the eligibility information directly into the system. The system is user friendly, making it simple for all employees—not just "techies"—to access the system. The system is based on *Status* software, available from C. P. International. While initial phases of the posting system are for exempt jobs only, the program is slated to expand to include hourly and salaried nonexempt positions.[13]

IDEA NO. 81: HIRING BONUSES

While hiring bonuses (also called sign-on bonuses) are not new, they are now being used with more frequency and for more varied recruitment needs. In one survey, all 15 companies contacted offered some sort of bonus, typically on a case-by-case basis. Another survey conducted by *The Fordyce Letter* reported 42 percent of 1,422 HR professionals offer some sort of hiring bonus.

Bonuses are generally restricted to upper-level management, hard-to-find positions, or professional occupations. The health care industry has seen a dramatic increase in the use of these bonuses.

Bonus amounts can range from $1,000 to $25,000, and are generally tied in some way to salary level. One rule of thumb says that for salaries up to the $100,000 level, a hiring bonus should be up to 10 percent; for salaries above this mark, the percentage can be greater.[14]

Pros and Cons of Bonuses

One of the biggest objections to hiring bonuses comes from current employees, who find it distasteful when they learn a new employee can earn thousands of dollars more in their first year, which can cause internal equity issues. Another concern is that job-hoppers, particularly in the hard-to-recruit nursing ranks, may find hiring bonuses attractive and be encouraged by this practice. In direct combat, some companies are paying out the bonus over a period of several years, offering incentives for retention.

One of the biggest benefits of a hiring bonus is that employers can entice new employees into accepting the new job without permanently impacting base salaries. It helps compensate employees for lost benefits when changing jobs.

Organizations considering the implementation of sign-on bonuses should develop specific guidelines for payment and should closely analyze internal-equity issues before initiating any program.

Hiring bonuses seem to be most effective when they are offered as a competitive benefit. This strategy may make your company more productive in reaching staffing goals, to the extent hiring bonuses are not being used by your competition.

Hiring bonuses aren't for top-salary jobs exclusively. One employer ran a help-wanted ad offering a $100 bonus for anyone hired as a result of the ad, with the bonus paid after 30 days. The ad didn't have to be run as often, saving money and drawing more responses.[15]

IDEA NO. 82: VIDEO

Why not replace traditional direct-mail letters and brochures with a recruitment video? Many companies are discovering that it takes a new approach to get the attention of the candidates today, and video is an appealing and accepted medium. Recruitment videos can also be shown at open houses, career and job fairs, information seminars, college/school recruiting, and other traditional recruitment activities.

Develop a professional video—either in-house or out-of-house—but use professionals who understand the medium. An amateurish approach will only create an image of a second-rate employer looking to cut costs.

IDEA NO. 83: CORPORATE LAYOFFS AND OUTPLACEMENT ORGANIZATIONS

Economic downturns can provide opportunities for employers surviving during hard times. Since many organizations offer displaced employees excellent outplacement services, recruiters can take advantage of this by working with the outplacing employer, or with the outplacement firm directly.

AT&T offers a "Job Access Hot Line," a free call-in service listing 40,000 jobs in its databank. General Motors and the United Auto Workers opened an employment center with a job bank for displaced workers. Stroh Brewery Company, after merging with Schlitz, provided services for its employees—placing 98 percent of their dislocated workers.[16]

IDEA NO. 84: COMPUTERIZED DATABASE RÉSUMÉ-RETRIEVAL SYSTEMS

A human resources executive from a large university recently discussed the organization's dilemma: many of the candidates applying for a specific open position could not be considered for other positions that became available a few months later because the university had no system in place to keep up with the large volume of applications and résumés. Many companies, because of this lost opportunity, are turning to the computer to store, track, and analyze applicant information on a database system.

Most systems have the capabilities of entering key applicant data and then sorting by certain criteria to discover candidates who meet position specifications. For example, an employer may wish to see if there are any applicants in the system with a bachelors degree in marketing, with three-to-five years of related experience, who are fluent in Japanese. By entering these criteria, the recruiter can determine how many, if any, current applicants meet selection requirements.

Most software programs have the capabilities to handle EEO (Equal Employment Opportunity) record-keeping information; many can also discard applications uniformly after a specified length of time. Systems can also be developed to keep in contact with applicants, writing thank-you letters and other applicant correspondence.

IDEA NO. 85: WALK-INS

One of the oldest methods in the recruitment book is to rely on walk-ins—candidates who come in and apply. While few recruiters rely exclusively on this method, it can be another source worthy of scrutiny.

To capitalize on walk-in activity, develop a system for uniformly and graciously greeting applicants. Roll out the red carpet: offer a beverage; offer to hang up a coat. Train the receptionist or whoever is responsible for greeting candidates on how to explain the employment process and what is involved. You may want to develop a one-page information sheet or recruitment brochure on procedures and how the process will work. Let candidates know if there are services to assist them, such as an employment hot line with a listing of open positions.

Respond to all applicants with courtesy, acknowledging receipt of their application/résumé, thanking them for their interest, and informing them of the next steps in the process. A "don't call us, we'll call you" attitude is inappropriate given the difficulties of finding qualified employees in a changing labor environment.

Ideas for More Updated Approaches

Idea No. 67: Hold an open house.

Idea No. 68: Take an open house on the road.

Idea No. 69: Participate in a career fair or job fair.

Idea No. 70: Plan an information seminar.

Idea No. 71: Using executive-search firms.

Idea No. 72: Working with recruitment agencies.

Idea No. 73: Develop compelling recruitment brochures and literature.

Idea No. 74: Develop a variety of recruitment collateral materials—T-shirts, bumper stickers, coffee mugs, buttons.

Idea No. 75: Create formal and informal employee-referral systems.

Idea No. 76: Tap into government-funded employment and training programs.

Idea No. 77: On-campus recruitment, other college recruiting ideas, and school-recruitment ideas.

Idea No. 78: Using trade publications and popular magazines for recruitment messages.

Idea No. 79: Networking and recruiting through trade and professional associations.

Idea No. 80: Manual and computerized in-house posting systems.

Idea No. 81: Hiring bonuses.

Idea No. 82: Video.

Idea No. 83: Corporate layoffs and outplacement organizations.

Idea No. 84: Computerized database résumé-retrieval systems.

Idea No. 85: Walk-ins.

Ideas for More Updated Approaches

Idea	Cost	Number People	Lead Time	Target
Idea No. 67: Open house	L–H	M	M–L	Y
Idea No. 68: Open house on the road	H	M	M–L	Y
Idea No. 69: Career/job fair	L–H	M	M–L	Y
Idea No. 70: Information seminar	L–H	M	M–L	Y
Idea No. 71: Search firms	H	—	M–L	Y
Idea No. 72: Recruitment agencies	H	—	M–L	Y
Idea No. 73: Brochures	M–H	M	M–L	Y
Idea No. 74: Collateral materials	M–H	M	M–L	N
Idea No. 75: Employee referrals	L–H	M	S–L	Y
Idea No. 76: Government programs	L	—	S–L	Y
Idea No. 77: School recruitment	L–H	—	M–L	Y
Idea No. 78: Publications	H	—	M–L	Y
Idea No. 79: Professional groups	L–H	—	M–L	Y
Idea No. 80: In-house posting	L–H	—	S–L	Y
Idea No. 81: Hiring bonuses	M–H	—	M–L	N
Idea No. 82: Video	H	M	L	Y
Idea No. 83: Corporate layoffs	L–M	—	S–L	N
Idea No. 84: Résumé database	H	M	S–L	Y
Idea No. 85: Walk-ins	L	—	S	N

Key:
Cost		Lead time	
Low	0–$200	Short	0–1 week
Medium	$200–$1,000	Moderate	1 week–4 weeks
High	$1,000+	Long	4+ weeks

Number people		Target	
Single	1	Yes	
Multiple	2 or more	No	
Either			

ENDNOTES

1. Jennifer J. Koch, "Open Houses: TV Ads Tell the Story," *Recruitment Today*, Winter 1990, pp. 6–15.
2. Ibid.
3. Tim Chauran, "Taking Texas on the Road," *Recruitment Today*, May/June 1989, pp. 48–52.

4. Margaret Magnus and Morton E. Grossman, "Job Fairs Are an Important Way to Recruit," *Recruitment Today*, Spring 1990, p. 43.

5. Jennifer J. Laabs, "The Hesitant Work Force," *Recruitment Today*, Summer 1990, pp. 42–45.

6. Gloria Glickstein and Donald C. Z. Ramer, "The Alternative Employment Marketplace," *Personnel Administrator*, February 1988, pp. 100–102.

7. Ibid.

8. Catherine D. Fyock, *America's Work Force Is Coming of Age: What Every Business Needs to Know to Recruit, Train, Manage, and Retain an Aging Work Force* (Lexington, Mass.: Lexington Books, 1990), pp. 76–77.

9. Catherine D. Fyock, *The Hiring Handbook* (Greenvale, N.Y.: Institute for Management 1988), pp. 106–107.

10. Ibid., p. 107

11. Jennifer J. Laabs, "The Captive Audience Advantage," *Recruitment Today*, Summer 1990, pp. 18–22.

12. "Bulletin Boards Are Effective Joblisting Tools," *Recruitment Today*, Fall 1990, p. 22.

13. Milan Moravec, "Effective Job Posting Fills Dual Needs," *HRMagazine*, September 1990, pp. 76–80.

14. Milton N. Dossin and Nancie L. Merritt, "Sign-On Bonuses Score for Recruiters," *HRMagazine*, March 1990, pp. 42–43.

15. David Ring, "Tips of the Month," *Communication Briefings*, June 1988, p. 1.

16. Gloria Glickstein and Donald C. Z. Ramer, "The Alternative Employment Marketplace," p. 101.

Chapter Seven

Image Management

T he best recruitment strategy in the world is only going to be marginally effective if the image and reputation of the organization is that of a poor place to work. Therefore, the best recruitment efforts will be conducted in conjunction with an image campaign, designed to show the public that the organization is a good place to work, and with a retention program, to ensure that the organization *is* a good place to work.

While many of the ideas presented in this book up to this point have been based upon marketing principles, the strategies outlined in this chapter are public relations-oriented, as well as product development- and customer service-oriented.

IDEA NO. 86: IMAGE ADVERTISING

Have you ever seen an ad that wasn't really a recruitment advertisement, and it wasn't really a product advertisement, but rather, something in between? That's what is known as image advertising, and many organizations are looking to this kind of image-building campaign as a means to attract both employees and customers.

The Saturn Corporation has undertaken an unusual image and product marketing approach that will undoubtedly bring in response from interested job prospects. In a two-page, four-color advertisement in *Time* magazine, the company runs a testimonial-type ad, featuring a quote from Alton Smith, a black tool and die maker:

> My best buddies in high school were twins. A couple of guys named Hugh and Hugo.
> We all had cars. And every Saturday we'd tear something down and put it back together just for the fun of it. So it's no big surprise that we all ended up in the car business.

But those guys wouldn't ever believe I just picked up and went to work for a car company that's never built a car before.

Well, what I'm doing now here at Saturn is something completely different.

Here, we don't have management and we don't have labor. We have teams. And we have what you call consensus. Everything's a group decision.

In the last seven months, I've only had a few days off here and there. But this is where I want to be. This is living heaven.

You work through breaks and you work through lunch. You're here all hours and even sometimes Saturdays. And you don't mind. Because no one's making you do it. It's just that here you can build cars the way you know they ought to be built.

I know the competition's stiff. I was out in California for a family reunion and everything was an import. Hondas, Toyotas. Well, now we're going to give people something else to buy.

I wouldn't be working all these hours if I didn't think we could. . . .

Even though this is also an image and marketing piece, it certainly does make a strong statement about the work environment offering something unique and important for its employees, making this a strong recruitment tool as well.

Toyota also understands the importance of national image advertising, and uses a two-page ad with the headline, "I'd like to thank my mother, my father and especially my fairy godmother." The statement is a quote from Karla Thomas, a black woman who is seen being crowned Miss Bethune-Cookman College. Karla was able to attend college through a scholarship from the United Negro College Fund, supported each year by Toyota.

The ad goes on to tell the reader that Toyota's involvement "has meant more than just financial support. Last summer, she was an intern at our Lexus division in California." The copy ends with the statement, "Through hard work and a little help from her friends, some of her wishes have already come true."

Toyota demonstrates its support of high school students in a similar ad campaign, featuring the headlines, "When they told us we were adopted we felt 10 feet tall."

The ad is about the Saxons, the high school basketball team for North High. As the ad tells us, the team, as well as the entire school, has been "adopted" by Toyota. Toyota provides scholarships and many types of support to the school, including the tutoring of students by Toyota employees and their participation in parent and teacher meetings.

The Burger King Corporation understands the importance of image to the parents and teachers—the influencers—of the many young people it has traditionally hired. In a 1990 half-page advertisement in *USA Today,* the company begins with, ''An open letter to the American people,'' with ad copy that reads:

> Burger King wishes to go on record as supporting traditional American values on television, especially the importance of the family.
> We believe the American people desire television programs that reflect the values they are trying to instill in their children.
> We pledge to support such programs with our advertising dollars.

Image advertising is also important in establishing the organization's reputation as a good place to work. Like product advertising in which the customer must see repeated messages before a decision is made to purchase the product, candidates don't usually wake up one morning, see an employment ad, and decide then and there to make a career change. The process of making that career-change decision is one that takes place over time, with the help of messages that come in the form of direct-recruitment advertising, product advertising, and image advertising, as well as word of mouth.

Thompson Recruitment Advertising Agency outlines a seven-step decision-making process for the typical candidate:

Step one: The honeymoon. During this stage, the individual is a newly hired employee and looks to advertising to confirm the wisdom of that decision.

Step two: Still basically happy. Although the employee is still satisfied with the current employer, the employee becomes more open to advertising messages from other organizations.

Step three: Happy, but not meeting expectations. In this stage, the employee begins to informally check out other employment opportunities, as the reality of the new job becomes apparent. Advertising will confirm the feeling that better opportunities are available.

Step four: Expectations raised. As the candidate casually views advertising, the expectations are raised about specific opportunities. At this point, the candidate becomes a prospect.

Step five: Action.   Advertising messages during this stage encourage the candidate to take action. Candidates will be most likely to respond to a request to call an 800 number or complete a "miniapplication" form.

Step six: Checking with peers in the network.   Before the candidate actually goes on an interview, the candidate talks with peers about the reputation of the prospective employer. Image advertising plays a role in not only encouraging the candidate, but in confirming the reputation of the employer with the peer group.

Step seven: The interview.   Based upon the interview as well as written recruitment literature and materials, the candidate will make the employment decision.[1]

Throughout this entire process, it is evident that confirmation, through image and direct-recruitment advertisement has an impact on not just the candidate as an active job seeker, but in the early stages when the candidate is still a happy employee, as well as the impact of image and recruitment advertising on peers within the candidate's network.

IDEA NO. 87: PUBLIC-RELATIONS COLLABORATION

Most corporate public relations departments have long been concerned with the image of the organization as a provider of goods and services to the community, but few have understood the importance of the image of the organization as an employer. Increasingly, however, human resources professionals are teaming up with these partners to create a public awareness about the organization as a good place to work.

Together, HR and PR departments are developing press releases and media campaigns, and are sponsoring local, regional, and national events to promote the organization in their role as employer.

Consider these joint activities your organization can develop:

- Send press releases on activities and programs your organization is sponsoring, such as new training programs, awards and incentives, and career ladders.
- Write human interest stories on individual employees—perhaps on an individual who did a good deed, or has been a volunteer for a charitable organization.

- Write stories about your organization, or about an executive with your organization, and send it to airline magazines, trade publications, and local newspapers.
- Sponsor a local or national event, such as the Special Olympic Games—particularly if you are interested in attracting persons with disabilities as part of your employment strategy. One food-service organization sponsored a national conference on the employment of older workers as a means to publicize their interest in this new targeted labor-market segment.
- Enter a contest that rewards employers for outstanding human resources programs.

Companies are exploring some unusual avenues for successfully promoting their organizations. The Sara Lee Corporation has created The Frontrunner Award to honor women of achievement in the fields of government, business, the arts, and the humanities. Sara Lee contributes $10,000 in the name of each Frontrunner to a not-for-profit women's organization. They publicize the award winners in each category in *Working Woman* magazine, with a full-page ad devoted to the winner in each category. While this advertisement is not a recruitment ad, it does send a strong signal to women as to Sara Lee's commitment to and recognition of women.

Ashton-Tate®, makers of *MultiMate*® software, sponsors a program each year in conjunction with *Working Woman* magazine, called the "Be Your Personal and Professional Best" contest. Contestants write an essay about how they benefit from the software, with the winner receiving a grand prize valued at over $11,000. Again, while not a recruitment-oriented program, the organization makes clear its role in supporting women in achieving their career goals.

In Louisville, Kentucky, *Business First,* the community's business publication, heralded a new community award, called "The 1990 Corporate Friend of the Family Awards," sponsored by the Family & Children's Agency. The awards are given in recognition of organizations' commitment to supporting employees' family well-being, including the sponsorship of programs such as EAPs (employee assistance programs), day cares, wellness programs, lecture series, and support groups. The receipt of such an award would certainly be an excellent way to communicate to the public the employer's commitment to employees, and to develop an outstanding reputation as a good place to work.

Organizations can also participate in low-cost means to demonstrate their commitment to employees, such as the U.S. Department of Labor's

LIFT Awards program (Labor Investing for Tomorrow). The program, initiated in 1990, awarded 16 employers throughout the United States. Employers may nominate themselves, or gain additional information on this award program, by contacting the Labor Department's office of the assistant secretary for policy.

Before embarking on an image campaign, organizations should carefully analyze their employment image, as well as their image as a community citizen to see if there are issues that need to be addressed or internal programs that should be added or deleted. Before bringing your organization to public awareness, ensure that the skeletons are out of the closet and that you have nothing to hide once the media becomes interested.

IDEA NO. 88: RECRUITMENT, RETENTION, AND THE ART OF SETTING REALISTIC CANDIDATE EXPECTATIONS

Customers define excellent customer service as having their needs and expectations met and exceeded. And so it is with employees: to keep them satisfied in the job, the employer must meet and exceed those job expectations. It then becomes an important retention element to appropriately sell the benefits of employment in such a way that employees will be satisfied when they do start on the new job. When candidates are oversold, they become dissatisfied because the job does not meet their expectations, and they leave the organization, causing a need to recruit again, as well as giving the organization a negative reputation as an employer that doesn't live up to promises.

Being a recruiter in competitive labor markets means that honesty must be foremost, even when the competition is overselling the benefits of employment. What should recruiters do to set realistic expectations? Here are some ideas:

- Present both the good and the bad issues of employment. If the work is hard and the hours are long—say so. If the work is challenging, but there are opportunities for growth and advancement—say that too. Provide an honest picture of what the job is like, not just the positives.
- Provide a tour of the job site to give the candidate a more realistic picture of what the day-in and day-out environment of the job is

like. This is particularly important in jobs in which applicants have
not seen the job duties being performed before, and when applicants are facing their first job in an industry or occupation.

- Permit current employees to talk with job candidates. Encourage
  them to offer a real-world view of the job satisfiers and job dis-
  satisfiers.
- Provide an employment tryout. Many employers work through
  temporary-help agencies so that the job candidate has a chance to see
  what the job is like before an offer is actually extended or accepted.
- Sell only those benefits the organization can deliver. Don't be
  tempted to promise what may not come true.

Mrs. Fields Cookies offers an "On the Job Experience" program, in
which retail-management candidates work for four hours performing
many of the job duties that will be experienced in the new job, such as mix-
ing dough, baking cookies, working the counter, and mopping floors. The
company pays them an hourly wage and gives them the opportunity to
really see what the job is like before accepting an offer.

Regional personnel manager Jeff Green feels that the program has
helped reduce turnover. He states, "Although approximately one third of
the applicants drop out of consideration after this experience, it is better to
have them leave now than three months after they have taken the job."[2]

IDEA NO. 89: RECRUITMENT, RETENTION, AND BUYER'S REMORSE IN POSTOFFER ACTIVITIES AND NEW-EMPLOYEE ORIENTATION

What is buyer's remorse? If you've ever made a major purchase, you probably know the feeling. You begin to wonder, "What have I done?" "Is
this a good buy?" "Did I do the right thing?" "Will I be happy with my
decision?"

Candidates who accept your offer of employment also begin to experience buyer's remorse, and wonder, "Have I made the right decision?"
"Will I be successful in the new job?" "Is this the right move for me right
now?" "Will I be happy?"

Keeping candidates happy beyond the offer is an important challenge to
recruiters today, with many employers reporting candidates who accept
the job offer, yet never show up for work on the hire date. Others report

that candidates show up for work, yet mysteriously leave and never return after lunch. Discussed here are strategies for keeping candidates involved through postoffer activities, and helping them avoid feelings of buyer's remorse through new-employee orientation strategies.

Postoffer Activities

Recruiters are developing creative ways to stay in touch with candidates during that time between the offer and the date of hire. Consider some of these activities to reassure candidates on their employment decision:

- Mail an offer letter, confirming the terms and conditions of employment, and welcoming the candidate to your organization. Or, if an offer letter is not appropriate, just send a letter or handwritten note welcoming candidates and congratulating them on their smart decision.
- Deliver a small gift to the candidate to say ''welcome aboard!''
- Send flowers with a note expressing your excitement about the candidate joining you. Some companies send flowers to the spouse or family members of relocating employees as a means to express excitement about the new opportunity.
- Invite the candidate to the work site for a tour, a meeting, or just another chance to review benefits and other pertinent information.
- Get together with the candidate for lunch as a means to discuss informal questions and issues of importance to the candidate.

New-Employee Orientation Programs

Design new-employee orientation programs with buyer's remorse in mind. Help the new employees see why their decision is a good one, through programs and activities that build rapport with co-workers and establish a bonding with the organization.

One source recommends adding a statement on ''Why We Hired You'' to orientation literature. Include subjects such as we have faith in you; you have potential; we want to see you succeed on the new job.[3]

Other ideas to improve the orientation process in order to reduce turnover and increase retention rates include the following:

- Develop a check list for new-employee orientation so that you won't forget important issues.

- Involve the employee in the orientation process. Let communications be a two-way street, not merely a lecture on policies, procedures, and benefits.
- Develop a buddy system, or mentoring program, for new employees. Permit employees who are interested to volunteer for this activity; forced volunteerism may defeat the purpose of such a system. Buddies, or mentors, can assist the new employee in learning the informal procedures and systems in the new work environment.
- Make sure that the new employee's direct supervisor is involved in the orientation process and has scheduled time to spend visiting.
- Check to ensure that the employee's work site is ready, with supplies ordered and a work station available.
- Make the orientation process just that, a process, not just a one-day indoctrination. Include orientation meetings, briefings, or lunches after one week, one month, and three months to more fully bond the new employee, and answer new questions that arise during this time period.
- Remember that the informal, social activities are just as important, if not more important, to the new employee who is establishing new relationships. Be sure to include the employee in informal get-togethers.

IDEA NO. 90: RECRUITMENT, RETENTION, AND THE ROLE OF LISTENING TO EMPLOYEES

When customers have a bad shopping experience, they spread the word to 10 to 20 of their friends. When employees have a bad employment experience, how many others do you think are told about this experience? While there isn't any current research on this yet, it could be estimated that employees literally tell everyone that they know and come in contact with!

Therefore, keeping current employees happy—meeting their needs and keeping them motivated—is an important part of recruitment. If your employees are badmouthing the organization, the most creative, innovative, dynamic recruitment program will not be effective, given the reputation of your organization.

How can employers tune in to the needs and concerns of their employees? There are many ways, both informal and formal, to find out if you are hitting or missing the mark. Listen through exit interviews, attitude surveys, management by wandering around (MBWA), open-door policies, and 50-50 meetings, all discussed below.

EXIT INTERVIEWS

Do you know why your employees are leaving your organization? At times when finding qualified employees becomes more difficult, discovering the reasons behind employee turnover becomes even more important.

Exit interviews can be conducted in three basic ways: face-to-face interview at the time of termination, questionnaire, and telephone interview. The face-to-face interview is more likely to result in some information shared, given management's commitment to allotting time for the interview. In-person interviews are also beneficial in that subtle clues can be discerned by the skilled interviewer by watching nonverbal signals, permitting the interviewer to probe into areas of concern. One drawback is that the terminating employee may feel threatened by this interview and may not want to burn any bridges until situated in the new job.

Questionnaires are an excellent alternative for employers who don't have the time or the expertise to conduct face-to-face interviews. Simple survey forms can be mailed to exited employees, to be returned in a pre-stamped envelope. The biggest problem with this format is the typical low response rate and inability to probe into areas of concern.

A telephone interview may be an attractive alternative for many employers. In this format, the company representative telephones the exited employee 30 to 90 days after the last day on the job, and asks follow-up questions. Usually the interviewer uses a structured interview form and asks for additional information when answers are vague or when this is deemed appropriate. This format is appealing to many employers in that it is easy to conduct, response rates are high, and the exited employee has had a long enough period of time in the new job to be frank about issues and concerns. Many employers are also using this opportunity to invite back those excellent performers who may have discovered that leaving the organization wasn't such a good idea.

Exit interviews should be conducted by someone other than the employee's supervisor so that information can be gathered on the effectiveness of management and the importance of this element in the decision to leave the organization. Generally, the company calls upon the human resource professional to handle this function, as it provides the objectivity of a third party, as well as someone trained in interviewing techniques.

Gather trend information to determine if the reason to leave the organization is a one-time, situational issue, or a trend of importance to the organization. One department, preferably the human resource department, should track and analyze these trends.

ATTITUDE SURVEYS

Attitude surveys can be an excellent way to gain the pulse of your employee opinions before they leave the organization. They can serve as a barometer of the atmosphere in the organization, serving as an early warning of problems to surface. Attitude surveys, when administered annually, can also give a picture of how the organization is doing from one year to the next.

An organization should only administer attitude surveys when management has made a clear commitment to act upon information received from the surveys. Once a survey has been administered, morale generally improves, since employees are feeling that management is really listening to their issues and concerns. Morale will plummet if management fails to act on the issues raised in the survey.

Ideally, the organization publishes survey results, in whole or in part, back to the employees participating, with specific action plans established. Some issues are identified as immediate-action issues, some as long-term issues; others will be identified as issues over which the organization has little control. These issues need to be properly identified with employees, with action plans outlined for issues within each category.

The organization should administer these surveys to employees during work time at the work site; otherwise, response rates will be low.

Surveys should be designed, just as the best customer service questionnaires are designed, not merely to ask, "How are we doing?" but, rather, to ask the better question, "What do you need?"

MBWA

MBWA—or "management by wandering around"—is now a term familiar to most managers who have read *In Search of Excellence*. MBWA is the management practice of keeping an eye and ear open to what is going on with employees, out in the field, in the plant, or in the office environment. It means that managers and supervisors need to get out of their offices and go where their employees are in order to understand what is really going on in the business.

MBWA means asking employees such questions as:

- How are you doing?
- What can I do for you?
- What do you need to do your job effectively?
- How can we make your job better/more productive/more efficient?
- How can we serve the customer (internal or external) more effectively?

By asking these questions, managers can get a handle on problems before they become issues that cause dissatisfaction, and ultimately, turnover.

OPEN-DOOR POLICIES

Are employees always welcome to bring in issues, problems, and concerns, without fear of retribution? Consider creating a climate that permits employees to feel free to bring issues to management's attention.

One hospital, experiencing high turnover among nurses, decided to develop an open-door program. Initially, this was difficult, in that nurses felt that management wasn't really interested in listening, or that they would be ostracized for bringing problems to management's attention. The human resource manager had to slowly develop trust, by carefully listening to problems and fully explaining policies, programs, and issues with nurses when they finally did bring up issues.

50–50 MEETINGS

Fifty-fifty meetings are those in which management speak their minds for half the time period, and employees speak up on issues of concern for the other half of the meeting. Many employers encourage employees to prepare written questions prior to this meeting, with management making a commitment to answer any and all questions.

Fifty-fifty meetings can be a part of all-employee meetings, small staff meetings, or any other employee gathering. One retailer decided to conduct breakfast meetings with small groups of employees each week. The retailer asked questions of employees, similar to those outlined in the MBWA section. As a result, the employees shared that they were concerned with the lack of lighting in the parking lot and that they were concerned with walking to their cars at night.

This particular store was having difficulties in staffing; it was becoming increasingly hard to find employees to work the closing shift.

As a result of the breakfast meeting, the employer installed additional lighting in the parking lot. Three benefits came to the company. The first was that the employees were ecstatic that management had not only asked for their input, but had acted on this information. Morale soared. The second benefit was that the closing shift, which had been so difficult to staff, was now easily staffed. The issue of lighting had, in fact, been a staffing issue. A third thing happened—customer count in the evening increased, as it had been a customer issue as well!

When the district management was asked about why this issue wasn't addressed earlier, they responded, ''Nobody told us.'' When the employees were asked why they had never raised this issue before, they answered, ''Nobody asked us.'' In fact, employees felt that they shouldn't raise issues, else they would be perceived by management as troublemakers. The point is, management must create the right climate to help employees know that their input is valuable.

IDEA NO. 91: EMPLOYEE PROGRAMS

Offering a work environment that is appealing to employees, and providing benefits that meet employees needs is a part of the marketing process, in that there must be product features, advantages, and benefits to offer to these employee/customers. Designing a product worthy to be sold to employees involves taking a close look at employee programs, to discover if you are offering your employees the right mix of benefits and opportunities that will meet their needs.

Consider these programs, and see which you are making available to your employees in the six categories outlined here:

1. **Competitive compensation package**
   - Gainsharing, bonuses, thrift plans, and other incentives that pay for performance.
   - Skill-based pay that pays for the skills possessed by the employee, not just for the work performed.
   - Broad banding, in which several pay grades are grouped together to permit greater salary ranges and increased opportunities for pay increases over time.
   - Cafeteria benefits, which allow employees to choose the benefits that they need most.
   - Paid time-off funds, so that employees have a set number of hours to use for sick time and personal time, without need to supply ''excuses'' (and so that employers don't have to police time off).
   - Performance-based incentives, so that employees who work harder receive more.
   - Decentralization of pay administration, giving the authority for pay decisions to those closest to the management issues.
   - Open communication of pay systems, letting all employees understand how the system works.
   - Level playing field, eliminating ''royalty'' and ''peon'' classifications, enhancing a cooperative work environment.
   - Broader-based employee ownership.
   - Direct linkages of pay for performance.

2. **Chance for growth and development**
   - Advancement opportunities and career ladders, giving all employees the chance to grow on the job.
   - Cross-training, permitting chances to move into other occupations.
   - In-house seminars.
   - In-house book clubs and other internal learning opportunities.
   - Pay for out-of-house seminars and conferences.
   - Educational assistance, including tuition-advance programs and tuition-reimbursement schemes.
   - Scholarships.
   - Sabbaticals to reward and rejuvenate those with tenure.
   - In-house libraries.
   - Subsidy of computers for personal use.

3. **Quality of work life—quality of home life**
   - Employee involvement and participation—including quality circles, work teams, employee committees, and suggestion programs.
   - Employee-scheduling opportunities—including part-time, temporary, consulting, job-sharing, telecommuting, flex scheduling, and other nontraditional arrangements.
   - Employee time off—including vacation, paid time off, holiday pay, child care.

4. **Respect for the individual—health and fitness**
   - Health facilities offered on premises.
   - Health club memberships or subsidy of memberships.
   - Health classes held on premises.
   - Nonsmoking policies.
   - Special clubs and support groups for weight control and smoking cessation.

5. **Recognition and rewards for performance**
   - Employee-of-the-month programs.
   - Awards banquets for outstanding performers in different categories.
   - Service awards programs.
   - Competitive events that challenge employees and stimulate high performance.
   - Sales awards, production awards, and bonuses.
   - Informal rewards, such as thank-you letters, small gifts, picnics, or other social gatherings.

6. **Fun at work**
   - ''Olympics'' competition.
   - Informal dress days.
   - Company parties and picnics.
   - Organizational clubs.
   - Vacation clubs.

For more information on these and other employee programs and activities that enhance retention and therefore improve recruitment capabilities, the following books are recommended for further reading:

- Robert Levering, *A Great Place to Work: What Makes Some Employers So Good (and Most So Bad)* (New York: Random House, 1988).

- Martin Yate, *Keeping the Best and Other Thoughts on Building a Super Competitive Workforce* (Holbrook, Mass.: Bob Adams, Inc., 1991).
- Roger E. Herman, *Keeping Good People: Strategies for Solving the Dilemma of the Decade* (Cleveland, Ohio: Oakhill Press, 1990).

Ideas for Image Management

Idea No. 86: Image advertising.

Idea No. 87: Public-relations collaboration.

Idea No. 88: Recruitment, retention, and the art of setting realistic candidate expectations.

Idea No. 89: Recruitment, retention, and buyer's remorse in postoffer activities and new-employee orientation.

Idea No. 90: Recruitment, retention, and the role of listening to employees.

Idea No. 91: Employee programs.

Ideas for Image Management

Idea	Cost	Number People	Lead Time	Target
Idea No. 86: Image advertising	H	M	L	Y
Idea No. 87: Public relations	L–H	M	L	N
Idea No. 88: Expectations	L	—	L	N
Idea No. 89: Postoffer activities	L	—	L	N
Idea No. 90: Listening	L–H	—	L	N
Idea No. 91: Employee programs	L–H	—	L	Y

Key:

Cost		Lead time	
Low	0–$200	Short	0–1 week
Medium	$200–$1,000	Moderate	1 week–4 weeks
High	$1,000+	Long	4+ weeks
Number people		Target	
Single	1	Yes	
Multiple	2 or more	No	
Either			

ENDNOTES

1. "Job Change: and Advertising's Role in Influencing Job Prospects," Thompson Recruitment Advertising Agency, pp. 1.1–2.2.
2. Dennis R. Laker, "Controlling Turnover," *Restaurant Personnel Management,* September 1990, pp. 1–2.
3. Gerald W. Young, "Tell Them Why," *communication briefings,* August 1989, p. 6.

Chapter Eight

Making It Work

H ow can you pull it all together into a formula that works for your organization? This chapter will help you in putting the various elements of recruitment planning together in order to develop a combination of recruitment activities and strategies that will assist you in meeting your staffing goals.

IDEA NO. 92: PREPARING YOUR SELLING PRESENTATION

What is it that your organization has to sell to prospective candidates? What are the features, advantages, and benefits of working with your organization, so that you can use those elements in developing recruitment messages for literature, advertising, and other collateral materials?

One of the best sources of information is within your organization. Conduct a poll of current employees, and ask them what they like most about working with the organization. Or, if you regularly conduct employee attitude/opinion surveys, the information may already be captured for you.

Some employers are initiating employee focus groups, with the assistance of marketing professionals, to carefully analyze the elements of the job that are appealing in order to construct advertising that captures those most important elements (refer to Chapter One's review of the Marriott Corporation's marketing approach).

Job applicants are another source of excellent information. Ask them what they want most in their next job and what they feel your organization can offer. Key in on these issues, because these are the issues that should be highlighted in your recruitment-advertising messages.

Brainstorm to discover what it is you have to offer. One hospital formed a team of nurses that became their recruitment and retention task force. With the assistance of an outside consultant, they were able to construct a list of the features of the hospital that could be "sold" to prospective candidates.

After you discover what the features are, the next step is translating those features into advantages and benefits. In other words, once you discover what you want to sell, you need to put it into words that relate directly to the needs and concerns of candidates—to show them "what's in it for me."

For example, it is not enough to say to candidates that your organization offers a tuition-advance program. That is merely stating the feature. To show the advantages and benefits—what's in it for me—tell candidates how the organization is committed to their success on the job, and that the company wants them to grow professionally, to advance, and to be successful. The organization's tuition-advance program helps each employee achieve these goals.

Another example is of an organization's state-of-the-art technology used in providing services, or in product design. To show candidates the advantages and benefits, the recruiter would explain that by having state-of-the-art facilities/products/services, employees are able to experience challenge, to be at the top of their profession, and to have specialized skills that will be in demand in the marketplace.

Employers will also need to consider how their list of features, advantages, and benefits stacks up against the competition for labor. Understand what your organization does uniquely well, and position those aspects as selling points to stress in the recruitment process.

One recruiter decided to develop such a listing and provided copies of this cheat sheet to all hiring managers who would be responsible for recruiting and interviewing candidates, so that everyone in the employment process could appropriately sell to candidates.

Increasingly, employers are also providing training for all managers involved in the recruitment and selection process. Too often, managers have been through training on the selection process, but have not received any information on the importance of selling the employment attributes.

IDEA NO. 93: TRACKING RECRUITMENT ACTIVITIES

For many organizations, recruitment budgeting has been a no-budget item, or a "spend what you need to get the job done" issue—especially for those companies that could easily rely on the numbers of baby boomers seeking employment. For many of these companies, very little was ever spent on recruitment, particularly for entry-level positions.

Increasingly, employers are having to spend more dollars, time, and energies on meeting staffing goals at all levels in the organization, and recruiters are having to be accountable for those resources allocated on various recruitment activities.

Recruiters are also carefully tracking recruitment data to ensure that resources are being used effectively. Outlined here are some of those measurements that should be utilized to determine recruitment productivity.

Cost per hire. Cost per hire is a relative measure of the effectiveness of recruitment activities. It can help recruiters understand the relative costs of hiring a semiskilled worker, a nurse, an entry-level retail clerk, an engineer, and an executive, to be used for budget purposes. You can use cost per hire to determine the effectiveness of specific recruitment activities, such as open houses, on-campus recruitment interviewing day, or a classified or display advertisement.

To calculate cost per hire, add all the costs associated with one hire, then divide by the total number of hires. For example, if the organization needs to fill three open positions and places two display advertisements in the Sunday metropolitan paper for a total cost of $3,000, and all three positions were filled, the cost per hire is $1,000 for each position.

Some organizations only include incremental costs in computing cost per hire, such as advertising costs, cost of collateral materials, travel costs for recruiters and applicants, room charges for open houses and recruitment events, recruitment agency fees, and the like. Others include overhead costs, such as the salaries of staff, office space, supplies, and so forth. The rule of thumb is to consistently collect data for cost-per-hire computations within your organization so that you will have an understanding of the relative costs of recruitment.

According to the fourth annual Society for Human Resource Management (SHRM)/Saratoga Institute Human Resources Effectiveness Report (HRER), the cost of hiring has increased each year. In 1989, the cost per hire was $8,049 for exempt positions, $1,000 higher than it was in 1987. In the past two years, nonexempt costs jumped from $456 to $803 in 1989.

Vacancy rates. Vacancy rates are a calculation of the total number of positions open, or vacant, as a percentage of the total number of positions. To calculate, divide the total number of positions by the number of vacant positions. Therefore, if your organization has 100 positions, with 10 positions vacant, the vacancy rate is 10 percent.

Vacancy rates permit recruiters to analyze how well they are doing to meet full staffing goals. Excessively high vacancy rates can also be an indication that cost-per-hire figures are too low. For example, if cost per hire has been maintained at too low a figure, with not enough budget dollars invested in recruitment, it can mean that positions are not being filled quickly enough, resulting in high vacancy rates.

Selection ratios.   Selection ratios help the recruiter analyze how many candidates are applying versus the number being selected for hire. Selection ratios give the recruiter an understanding of how effective the recruitment activity or message is in attracting qualified candidates.

To calculate selection ratios, add the number of candidates applying for a position, as a percentage of those actually selected for hire. For example, if there are 20 candidates for one hire, the selection ratio is 20:1, or 5 percent.

Selection ratios are helpful to the recruiter in developing a balance in attracting sufficient numbers of applicants for an open position, versus having only qualified candidates applying.

Retention rates/turnover rates.   Looking at turnover rates, or the reverse of turnover—retention—rates, recruiters can gain an understanding beyond their efficiency in filling open positions—their effectiveness in the employment process.

Turnover is calculated by dividing the number of those employees exiting the organization by the total number of employees. Therefore, if you have 100 employees, and 10 leave during the course of the year, the annual turnover rate is 10 percent.

Retention rates are calculated by determining the number of employees who stay during the year, divided by the total number of employees. So, if you have 100 employees, and 90 remain with the organization over the course of the year, the annual retention rate is 90 percent.

Retention rates, or turnover rates, are important for the recruiter to analyze, especially against specific recruitment activities. For example, an organization might find that it can recruit and hire many college graduates, but that the retention rate for this group of hires is significantly lower than for other recruitment activities targeted at different candidates.

Retention and turnover rates should also be analyzed with cost-per-hire data. It could be that cost-per-hire figures are too low for the overall effectiveness of the employment program. For example, you might learn that career fairs yield a low cost per hire, but that this activity yields low retention rates.

Affirmative action data.   For affirmative-action purposes, you should document all applicant demographic information. Recruiters should track this information for completing affirmative-action plans and for evaluating recruitment effectiveness in attracting a diversity of candidates representative of the labor market.

IDEA NO. 94: GETTING TOP-MANAGEMENT SUPPORT

To get top-management commitment and support of recruitment activities, as well as corresponding budget, staffing, and resource needs, human resource professionals may want to explore these ideas:

* Publish recruitment and retention data on a regular basis, such as cost per hire, turnover and retention rates, vacancy rates, and selection ratios to make top management aware of recruitment efforts.
* Share articles that document labor-shortage issues, and case studies on what organizations are doing to successfully meet employment needs.
* Write position papers on staffing and employment issues, highlighting the particular staffing challenges for your organization and recommendations for meeting those challenges.
* Report on benefits to the organization when employee staffing is improved. For example, when there is full staffing and customers are more satisfied with the service they receive, document this information in a report to management.
* Develop a recruitment-action plan, and regularly report on the status of this plan to top management.

IDEA NO. 95: GAINING TOTAL MANAGEMENT SUPPORT

It's not enough to have the support of top management; all levels of management must be committed to addressing the challenges of meeting full-staffing goals. In many organizations, the human resource department is seen as the only department responsible for meeting staffing needs, and what results is a ''go-fetch'' mentality—with human resources finding people whenever hiring managers have an open position.

To be effective, all levels of management must see their role in meeting staffing needs. Human resource professionals can be a resource to assist hiring managers, but cannot be solely responsible.

One company's human resource department, for example, wanted to focus on the increased employment of older workers as a means to meet recruitment needs. Top management had already blessed the project, and human resource recruiters were already referring qualified older candidates to the hiring managers. Suddenly, the hiring managers became ''too busy'' to conduct interviews, and the entire initiative came to a screeching halt.

What happened next was a meeting with the hiring managers, to discuss the importance of looking to various labor-market segments to meet their staffing needs. As it turned out, these managers held many preconceived notions about what older workers could and couldn't do and needed some additional information on the successes in employing older workers within the industry. After the meeting, managers were more open to the idea, and the program was eventually a success.

Consider various methods to gain the total management support of recruitment activities and strategies as outlined here:

- Prepare reports on staffing issues of importance to hiring managers.

- Establish a task force to address staffing issues. Call upon members from different departments, in varying levels of the organization.

- Initiate a suggestion system for employees to offer ideas on meeting staffing needs.

- Provide sensitivity training to managers on the issues of managing diversity, as well as recruiting diverse employees.

- Hold managers accountable for staffing issues in their departments. Include a goal for retention for every manager's performance, and tie achievement of that goal with pay increases and bonuses.

- Invite managers to participate in recruitment activities, such as open houses, career fairs, on-campus interviewing days, presentations to clubs and organizations, and information seminars.

IDEA NO. 96: DEVELOPING RECRUITMENT AND RETENTION TASK FORCES

One of the best methods to involve all levels of management in achieving staffing goals is the development of a recruitment and retention task force. Task forces can be strictly for a specific hard-to-recruit position, such as nursing, or can be formed to attack problems facing the organization as a whole.

When Suzanne Sutter, senior vice president of organizational planning and development for Cole National Corporation, studied the work-force projections and trends in 1988, she realized that the changes in the workplace were going to have a major impact on her company. Cole National is a retailing conglomerate, based in Cleveland, Ohio, comprised of such businesses as the optical department at Sears and Montgomery Wards, Things Remembered, and the gift and key shops at Sears and Wards.

Sutter determined that recruiting and retaining employees would be a key business issue for the 1990s, and developed a recruitment and retention task force made up of presidents, human resource executives and managers, and operations executives and managers. Their mission was to develop new ways of recruiting and retaining people—to share and "steal" ideas to make this happen, with equal emphasis on recruitment and retention. "I see quality staffing as the survival issue for this decade," states Sutter, "and I'm determined that Cole is going to be not just a survivor, but a winner!"

Sutter meets with the task force twice each year. The focus for retention was to think of employees as customers—and keep them happy with customer service strategies. Why? Says Sutter, "Our ability at Cole to deliver great service to our customers depends upon our ability to acquire and retain top-notch employees." The task force then focused on understanding the causes of turnover and the opportunity of retention, through a thorough analysis of turnover rates, exit interview results, and annual attitude surveys. At one of the corporation's divisions, for example, the task force gave management a comprehensive attitude survey.

Based on the results of these surveys, interviews, and statistics, they developed and implemented action plans with the focus on making a difference within each division.

Recruitment was also a major focus, with the key philosophy of using a marketing approach with the employee as the customer. Task-force members were challenged to experiment with new methods to acquire employees and to develop systems to make quality selection decisions.

The results of Sutter's emphasis on staffing have been tremendous, with very favorable outcomes, notes Sutter. At one division alone, with an emphasis on reducing turnover of seasonal employees, turnover was decreased by 13 percent in 1988, by 10 percent in 1989, and by a whopping 100 percent in 1990. "What it really amounted to was the care and feeding of our people," comments Sutter, with care translating into daily team meetings, and a change in thinking about the importance of seasonal employees to the operation.

Other divisions also boast dramatic results. Cole Key has seen reductions in turnover in 1990 of 31 percent—but only when employee retention was seen as a key business goal. In the preceding year, for example, the operation saw an 18 percent increase in turnover when it failed to stress the importance of employee retention.

Sutter is increasingly convinced that by making the staffing issue a major business goal for all levels in the organization, Cole can continue to position itself as a leader in the industry.[1]

IDEA NO. 97: DEVELOPING YOUR RECRUITMENT-ACTION PLAN

The first step in developing a recruitment-action plan is to project staffing needs for the year, based upon experience from previous years, coupled with an understanding of the business needs for the upcoming year. Once staffing needs are projected for the year, identify monthly needs as accurately as possible.

With this information in hand, identify the complete recruitment-action plan, taking into consideration the labor-market segments to be identified for recruitment purposes (based upon affirmative-action goals, diversity needs, as well as informal identification of segments that have been underutilized or not targeted for recruitment in the past). Once the market segments are identified, then you can design recruitment messages and activities to meet the needs of the target population.

Consider ways to update past recruitment practices, and include new ideas and strategies. Think about the role of geographic boundaries and how candidates can be recruited beyond those boundaries. Also, realize the role of image and retention in the process.

Finally, review the action plan against past measures of recruitment productivity (cost per hire, vacancy rates, and turnover and retention rates) to determine which activities and messages are most effective in meeting staffing needs. Be sure also to analyze the action plan to ensure that it is consistent with the recruitment principles outlined in Chapter One, as well as the measures outlined in this chapter.

IDEA NO. 98: LOOKING INTO STAFFING ALTERNATIVES

Sometimes the traditional method of meeting staffing needs just doesn't work. Increasingly, full-time, permanent positions are "dinosaur" terms, states management consultant and staffing alternatives expert, Gil Gordon, president of Gil Gordon Associates in Monmouth Junction, New Jersey.

As a means to attract more qualified candidates, employers are beginning to offer staffing alternatives, such as part-time work, flextime, peak-time scheduling, job sharing, telecommuting, and compressed work weeks.

First, here is a brief definition of terms:

- **Part-time** employees work less than a full schedule, usually 30 hours or less.

- **Flextime** permits employees to select the times of day they work, usually around a "core" time period in which all employees are on the job.

- **Peak-time scheduling** usually offers a premium wage for employees willing to work part-time during peak need times, such as the lunch rush in food service, and on Fridays for banking.

- **Job sharing** is the splitting of one full-time job into two part-time positions, with a mutual sharing of responsibilities between the job sharers.

- **Telecommuting** is an arrangement in which employees work out of their homes one or more days each week, usually through the use of telecommunications equipment, such as the telephone, facsimile machine, computers, and modems.

- **Compressed work weeks** involve a schedule of full-time hours (sometimes less than full-time hours for full-time pay) in less than a traditional five-day week, such as four 10-hour days each week or two 12-hour shifts.

Each of these alternative work schedules can be appealing to new groups of candidates who might not otherwise have found employment with your organization appealing. Some labor-market segments finding these alternative schedules attractive include:

- **Older workers** who want to have more leisure time for relaxation, travel, and time with grandchildren, and who have other forms of income.
- **Students** who need time for studies.
- **Back-to-work mothers, dual-career couples, and single parents** who are trying to balance work and home responsibilities.

Gordon believes that providing staffing alternatives will permit employers, especially those savvy enough to offer alternatives before their labor competitors, a marketing niche that will permit them to attract many qualified candidates.

Gordon also proposes that employers, especially those facing staffing challenges, may want to expand their use of alternative staffing schedules while decreasing their use of full-time traditional workers. This staffing mix affords the employer more staffing flexibility, while offering employees schedules more likely to meet their increasingly diverse needs. He encourages employers not to do the "same thing for everyone," but rather, to do "some thing for everyone."[2]

IDEA NO. 99: MAKING IT WORK—MORE RECRUITING PRINCIPLES

To make recruitment effective today and to achieve staffing goals, here are three additional principles for designing a recruitment plan.

ONGOING RECRUITMENT EFFORTS

The lead time for filling positions is increasing. Positions that took one week to fill may take several weeks or a month to fill today. Similarly, the more difficult searches taking one month or more to complete now may last three months, six months, or longer. One employer searching for a highly specialized technical worker confided that their search had been going on for over 18 months.

With these kinds of lead times in mind, employers must not wait until the last minute—when the opening occurs—to begin the search process. In fact, many organizations are beginning to think towards the creation of an employment "pool" of qualified candidates who are in queue for upcoming positions.

How do you keep candidates interested in remaining in the pool? One of the first considerations is to avoid recruiting those who are out of work. These individuals will need employment immediately and will not wait while the opportunity within your organization arises, but will probably take the first reasonable offer of employment. Therefore, employers seeking to build a pool should avoid strategies that tend to attract the unemployed, strategies such as advertising in help-wanted sections of the paper. Instead, focus on intrusive forms of recruitment advertising that appeal to those individuals who are happily working someplace else.

Another means to keep candidates in the pool is to keep in touch with candidates through some structured process. Consider a correspondence approach, with a different, personalized letter mailed to each candidate each month, or other appropriate time period. For example, at time period one, all candidates receive a letter; at the end of time period two, all candidates still in the pool receive form letter two. You can personalize each letter through word processing technologies. In fact, many résumé software programs contain correspondence options.

You can contact candidates by telephone to update them on their status. Telegrams are another means to send the message with impact. You could also send small gifts or giveaways to candidates to encourage their continued interest in the company.

MULTIFACETED PLAN OF ATTACK

Don't rely on any one method to achieve your staffing goals. Continue to try different activities and messages, and track the effectiveness of each. Look at different labor-market segments that have traditionally not been targeted by your organization.

Consider using a multimedia, blitz approach to dramatically increase awareness about your organization and to get results from recruitment events.

Enlist all management and employees in your organization to assist you in the search for qualified candidates. It can't be done alone!

ADAPT

There have been many ideas presented throughout this book. Hopefully, you will be able to immediately use some of them to meet your staffing needs. However, some ideas may need to be modified to capitalize on your unique situation and to meet your unique needs.

Develop a proactive approach to recruitment marketing, and consider how you can use your own strengths as an employer to compete effectively with your competition for labor. Consider how traditional methods can be updated and modified to reap staffing results.

SUMMARY

Recruitment today is one of the most exciting, challenging components of running a business and will continue to be one of the top competitive issues for the 1990s and beyond. If organizations cannot attract and recruit top employees to meet staffing needs, they will be doomed to mediocrity and, ultimately, failure, because it is our employees who are the lifeblood of our organizations.

Ideas for Making It Work

Idea No. 92: Preparing your selling presentation.

Idea No. 93: Tracking recruitment activities.

Idea No. 94: Getting top-management support.

Idea No. 95: Gaining total management support.

Idea No. 96: Developing recruitment and retention task forces.

Idea No. 97: Developing your recruitment-action plan.

Idea No. 98: Looking into staffing alternatives.

Idea No. 99: Making it work—more recruiting principles.

Ideas for Making It Work

Idea	Cost	Number People	Lead Time	Target
Idea No. 92: Selling	L	—	S–L	N
Idea No. 93: Tracking	L	—	S–L	N
Idea No. 94: Top management	L	—	S–L	N
Idea No. 95: Total management	L	—	S–L	N
Idea No. 96: Task forces	L	—	S–L	N
Idea No. 97: Action plan	L	—	S–L	N
Idea No. 98: Staffing alternatives	L–H	—	S–L	N
Idea No. 99: Recruiting principles	L	—	S–L	N

Key:

Cost		Lead time	
Low	0–$200	Short	0–1 week
Medium	$200–$1,000	Moderate	1 week–4 weeks
High	$1,000+	Long	4+ weeks

Number people		Target	
Single	1	Yes	
Multiple	2 or more	No	
Either			

ENDNOTES

1. Catherine D. Fyock, ''Cole National's Suzanne Sutter Sees Employees as Customers,'' *Staffing 2000,* March–April 1991, p. 3.
2. Gil Gordon, Gil Gordon Associates, from a presentation April 9, 1991, at the Kentucky Society for Human Resource Management Conference.

Appendix

Resources to Make It Work

Listed here are agencies and programs offering employment and training services and information to employers seeking qualified candidates.

OLDER WORKER PROGRAMS

AARP
1909 K Street NW
Washington, DC 20049
(202) 872-4700

Aging/Adult Services Administration
OB-44A
Olympia, WA 98504
(206) 586-3768

Aging and Adult Administration
1789 West Jefferson
Phoenix, AZ 85007
(602) 542-4446

Aging and Adult Service
1575 Sherman St. 4th Floor
Denver, CO 80203-1714
(303) 866-3851

Aging in America
1500 Pelham Parkway
Bronx, NY 10461
(212) 824-4004 (inside N.Y. state)
(800) 845-6900 (outside N.Y. state)

Aging Services
State Capitol Building
Bismark, ND 58505
(701) 224-2577

Aging Services Division
P.O. Box 25352
Oklahoma City, OK 73125
(405) 521-2327

Alliance for Aging Research
2021 K Street NW #305
Washington, DC 20006
(202) 293-2856

American Society on Aging
833 Market Street #512
San Francisco, CA 94103
(415) 543-2617

Board on Aging
444 Lafayette Rd. 4th Floor
St. Paul, MN 55155-3843
(612) 296-2770

Bureau of Elder/Adult Services
State House, Station #11
Augusta, ME 04333
(207) 624-5335

Bureau on Aging
217 S. Hamilton St., Suite 300
Madison, WI 53703
(608) 266-2536

Center for Understanding Aging
Framingham State College
Framingham, MA 01701
(508) 626-4979

Columbia University
622 W. 113th Street
New York, NY 10025
(212) 854-4158

Commission on Aging
770 Washington Avenue #470
Montgomery, AL 36130
(205) 242-5743

Commission on Aging
400 Arbor Lake Drive
Columbia, SC 29223
(803) 735-0210

Commission on Aging
706 Church St., Suite 201
Nashville, TN 37243-0860
(615) 741-2056

Commission on Aging
Holly Grove, State Capitol
Charleston, WV 25305
(304) 348-3317

Department for the Aging
700 East Franklin Street
Richmond, VA 23219-2327
(804) 225-2271

Department of Aging
1600 K Street
Sacramento, CA 95814
(916) 322-5290

Department of Aging
50 W. Broad Street, 9th Floor
Columbus, OH 43266-0501
(614) 466-5500

Department of Aging
231 State Street
Harrisburg, PA 17101-1195
(717) 783-1828

Department of Aging and Disabilities
103 South Main Street
Waterbury, VT 05676
(802) 241-2400

Department of Elder Affairs
914 Grand Avenue
Des Moines, IA 50319
(515) 281-5187

Department of Elderly Affairs
160 Pine Street
Providence, RI 02903-3708
(401) 277-2858

Department of Family Services
P.O. Box 8005
Helena, MT 59604
(406) 444-5900

Department on Aging
175 Main Street
Hartford, CT 06106
(203) 566-3238

Department on Aging
421 East Capitol Avenue
Springfield, IL 62701
(217) 785-2870

Department on Aging
915 S.W. Harrison
Topeka, KS 66612-1500
(913) 296-4986

Department on Aging
P.O. Box 95044
Lincoln, NE 68509
(402) 471-2306

Department on Aging
P.O. Box 12786 Capitol Station
Austin, TX 78741-3702
(512) 444-2727

Division for Aging Services
340 North 11th Street
Las Vegas, NV 89101
(702) 486-3545

Division of Aging
1901 N. DuPont Highway
New Castle, DE 19720
(302) 421-6791

Division of Aging
Caller Box 29531
Raleigh, NC 27626-0531
(919) 733-3983

Division of Aging
Hathaway Building, Room 139
Cheyenne, WY 82002-0480
(307) 777-7986

Division of Aging/Adult Services
Box 45500
Salt Lake City, UT 84145-0500
(801) 538-3910

Division of Aging and Adult Services
P.O. Box 1437
Little Rock, AR 72203-1437
(501) 682-2441

Division of Aging and Adult Services
421 W. Pascagoula Street
Jackson, MS 39203
(601) 949-2070

Division of Aging Services
P.O. Box 7083
Indianapolis, IN 46207-7083
(317) 232-7020

Division of Aging Services
275 East Main Street, 6 West
Frankfort, KY 40621
(502) 564-6930

Division of Elderly/Adult Services
6 Hazen Drive
Concord, NH 03301-6501
(603) 271-4680

Division of Senior Citizens
P.O. Box 2816
Agana, Guam 96910

Division on Aging
P.O. Box 1337
Jefferson City, MO 65102
(314) 751-3082

Division on Aging
S. Broad and Front Sts., CN807
Trenton, NJ 08625-0807
(609) 292-4833

E E O C
1801 L Street NW
Washington, DC 20507
(800) USA-EEOC

Executive Office/Elder Affairs
38 Chauncy Street
Boston, MA 02111
(617) 727-7750

Executive Office on Aging
335 Merchant St., Room 241
Honolulu, HI 96813
(808) 548-2593

Green Thumb Inc.
2000 N. 14th Street #800
Arlington, VA 22201
(703) 522-7272

National Caucus/Center/Black Aged
1424 K Street NW #500
Washington, DC 20005
(202) 637-8400

National Committee for Employment
1522 K Street NW, Suite 300
Washington, DC 20005

National Council on the Aging
409 Third St. SW, Suite 200
Washington, DC 20024
(202) 479-1200

National Council/Senior Citizens
1331 F Street NW
Washington, DC 20004-1171
(202) 347-8800

National Displaced Homemakers Network
1411 K Street NW #930
Washington, DC 20005
(202) 628-6767

National Indian Council/Aging
6400 Uptown Blvd. NE #510-W
Albuquerque, NM 87110
(505) 888-3302

National Urban League
500 East 62nd Street
New York, NY 10021
(212) 310-9210

Office Adult Services/Aging
700 North Illinois Street
Pierre, SD 57501
(605) 773-3656

Office for Elderly Affairs
Ponce De Leon Ave. #1603
San Ture, PR 00908
(809) 721-5710

Office for the Aging
N.Y. State Plaza, Bldg. #2
Albany, NY 12223
(518) 474-4425

Office of Aging
878 Peachtree St. NE, Room 632
Atlanta, GA 30309
(404) 894-5333

Office of Elderly Affairs
P.O. Box 80374
Baton Rouge, LA 70898-0374
(504) 925-1700

Office of Services to the Aging
P.O. Box 30026
Lansing, MI 48909
(517) 373-8230

Office on Aging
1424 K St. NW, 2nd Floor
Washington, DC 20005
(202) 724-5626

Office on Aging
Room 108, Statehouse
Boise, ID 83720
(208) 334-3833

Office on Aging
301 W. Preston St., Room 1004
Baltimore, MD 21201
(301) 225-1100

Older Alaskans Commission
Pouch C-Mail Station 0209
Juneau, AK 99811-0209
(907) 465-3250

Older Women's League
730 Eleventh St. NW #300
Washington, DC 20001
(202) 783-6686

Pacific/Asian Center/Aging
1511 Third Ave. #914
Seattle, WA 98101
(206) 448-0313

Program Office/Aging/Adult Services
1317 Winewood Boulevard
Tallahassee, FL 32301
(904) 488-8922

Senior Citizen Affairs
#19 Estate Diamond Frederiksted
St. Croix, VI 00840
(809) 772-4950 ext. 46

Senior Services Division
313 Public Service Building
Salem, OR 97310
(503) 378-4728

Special Committee on Aging
Room G-31 DSOB
Washington, DC 20510

State Agency on Aging
224 E. Palace Ave., 4th Floor
Santa Fe, NM 87501
(505) 827-7640

U.S. Department of Labor
200 Constitution Ave. NW #N-4643
Washington, DC 20210
(202) 535-0521

Wider Opportunities for Women
1325 G St. NW, Lower Level
Washington, DC 20005
(202) 638-3143

EMPLOYMENT PROGRAMS FOR PERSONS WITH DISABILITIES

ADA Guide-Resources Policy #0230
1615 H Street NW
Washington, DC 20062
(800) 638-6582 / (800) 352-1450 in MD

Administration on Developmental Disabilities
200 Independence Ave. SW, Room 358F
Washington, DC 20201
(202) 245-2888

Alexander Graham Bell Association for the Deaf
3417 Volta Place NW
Washington, DC 20007
(202) 337-5220 (V/TDD)

American Council of the Blind
1155 15th Street NW, Suite 720
Washington, DC 20005
(800) 424-8666

Association of Retarded Citizens of the United States
2501 Avenue J
Arlington, TX 76005
(817) 640-0204

Disabled American Veterans
807 Maine Avenue SW
Washington, DC 20024
(202) 554-3501

Epilepsy Foundation of America
4351 Garden City Drive
Landover, MD 20785
(301) 459-3700

Federal JOB Information Center
1900 E. Street NW
Washington, DC 20415
(202) 606-2700

Handicapped Student Service Programs
Box 21192
Columbus, OH 43221
(614) 488-4972 (V/TDD)

IBM National Support Center for Persons with Disabilities
Box 2150, HO6RI
Atlanta, GA 30301-2150
(800) 426-2133

Job Accommodation Network (JAN)
WVU, 809 Allen Hall
Morgantown, WV 26506-6123
(800) JAN-7234 (V/TDD)

Learning Disabilities Association of America
4156 Library Road
Pittsburgh, PA 15234
(412) 341-1515

Little People of America
P.O. Box 9897
Washington, DC 20016
(301) 589-0730

Mainstream Inc.
1030 15th Street NW, Suite 1010
Washington, DC 20005
(202) 898-1400

Muscular Dystrophy Association
810 Seventh Avenue
New York, NY 10019
(212) 586-0808

National Association of Rehabilitation Facilities (NARF)
P.O. Box 17675
Washington, DC 20041
(703) 648-9300

National Association of the Deaf
814 Thayer Avenue
Silver Spring, MD 20910-4500
(301) 587-1788

National Center for Disability Services
201 I.U. Willets Road
Albertson, NY 11507-1599
(516) 747-6323

National Council on Disability
800 Independence Ave. SW, Suite 814
Washington, DC 20591
(202) 267-3232

National Federation of the Blind
1800 Johnson Street
Baltimore, MD 21230
(301) 659-9314

National Multiple Sclerosis Society
205 East 42nd Street.
New York, NY 10017
(212) 986-3240

National Spinal Cord Injury Association
600 West Cummings Park #2000
Woburn, MA 01801
(617) 935-2722

Paralyzed Veterans of America
801 Eighteenth Street NW
Washington, DC 20006
(202) 872-1300

President's Commission on Mental Retardation
330 Independence Ave. SW, Room 5325
Washington, DC 20201
(202) 619-0634

President's Committee on Employment of People with Disabilities
1111 20th Street NW, Suite 636
Washington, DC 20036-3470
(202) 653-5044

Self Help/Hard of Hearing People
7800 Wisconsin Avenue
Bethesda, MD 20814
(301) 657-2248

Social Security Administration
Baltimore, MD 21235
(301) 876-6450

U.S. Department of the Treasury–IRS
Office of the Chief Counsel
Washington, DC 20224
(202) 566-4473

United Cerebral Palsy Association
1522 K Street NW #1112
Washington, DC 20005
(202) 842-1266

DISPLACED HOMEMAKER NETWORK

Alaska Women's Resource Center
111 West 9th Avenue
Anchorage, AK 99501
(907) 276-0528

Assisting People in Transition
2020 Riverside Drive
Berlin, NH 03584
(603) 752-1113

Career Center—YWCA
720 W. Washington Street
Boise, ID 83702
(208) 336-7306

Career Opportunities Project
P.O. Box 1266
Bloomington, IN 47402
(812) 332-3777

Career Transition
6500 Pacific Boulevard SW
Albany, OR 97321
(503) 967-6112

Center for Displaced Homemakers
7393 Florida Blvd.
Baton Rouge, LA 70806
(504) 925-6922

Center for New Directions
1430 North Second Street
Phoenix, AZ 85004
(602) 252-0918

Choices: Career Development Center
103 West Park
Bald Knob, AR 72010
(501) 724-6306

Creative Employment Projects
226 West Breckinridge Street
Louisville, KY 40203
(502) 581-7237

Displaced Homemaker Program
P.O. Box 797
Alpena, MI 49707
(517) 356-6569

Displaced Homemaker Program
523 Lake Avenue
Asbury Park, NJ 07712
(908) 776-2668

Displaced Homemaker Program
147 Park Street
Akron, OH 44308
(216) 253-5142

Displaced Homemaker Program
550 East 300 South
Kaysville, UT 84037
(801) 546-4134

Displaced Homemaker Program
P.O. Drawer 1127
Dublin, VA 24084
(703) 674-3600 x350

Displaced Homemaker Program
15 Ayers Street
Barre, VT 05641
(802) 479-1053

Displaced Homemaker
Program—YWCA
167 Duke of Gloucester Street
Annapolis, MD 21401
(301) 269-0378

Displaced Homemakers Program
2601 Carson Road
Birmingham, AL 35215
(205) 867-4832

Displaced Homemakers Program
Box 400
Calmar, IA 52132
(319) 562-3263

Displaced Homemakers Program
Stoddard House, University of Maine
Augusta, ME 04330
(207) 621-3440

Displaced Homemakers Program
2601 N.E. Barry Road
Kansas City, MO 64156
(816) 436-6500

Displaced Homemakers Program
487 N. Union Extension
Canton, MS 39046
(601) 859-3925

Displaced Homemakers Program
4001 Indian School Road NE #220
Albuquerque, NM 87110
(505) 841-4662

Displaced Homemakers Program
1121 North Spurgeon
Altus, OK 73521
(405) 477-2439

Displaced Homemakers Program
P.O. Box 447
Amarillo, TX 79178
(806) 371-5450

Displaced Homemakers
Program—YWCA
753 Fairfield Avenue
Bridgeport, CT 06604
(203) 334-6154

Displaced Homemakers
Program—YWCA
909 Wyoming Avenue
Billings, MT 59101
(406) 245-6879

Displaced Homemakers
Program—YWCA
234 East Third
Grand Island, NE 68801
(308) 384-8170

**Employment and Training
Program—YWCA**
1608 Woodmont Blvd.
Nashville, TN 37215
(615) 269-9922

Empowerment Program
1245 E. Colfax Avenue #404
Denver, CO 80218
(303) 863-7817

N.Y. Women's Employment Center
198 Broadway, Suite 200
New York, NY 10038
(212) 964-8934

**New Careers—Working
Opportunities for Women**
2700 University Ave. #120
St. Paul, MN 55114
(612) 647-9961

Project "Change"
1500 Fourth Avenue
Altoona, PA 16602
(814) 946-8454

Single Parent/DH Program
Route 12, Box 1273
Valdosta, GA 31602
(912) 333-2100

Single Parent/Homemaker Program
4302 Diamond Head Road
Honolulu, HI 96816
(808) 734-9500

Single Parent/Homemaker Program
125 South 2nd
Arkansas City, KS 67005
(316) 442-0430

Single Parent/Homemaker Program
2201 West Nye Lane
Carson City, NV 89703
(702) 887-3000

Single Parent/Homemaker Program
165 St. Philip St.
Charleston, SC 29413
(803) 723-7138

Single Parent/Homemaker Program
P.O. Box 1571
Aberdeen, SD 57401
(605) 622-2298

**Single Parent/Homemakers
Program**
222 West Bowen
Bismarck, ND 58504
(701) 221-3790

Single Parent Program
70 Metropolitan Avenue
Cranston, RI 02920
(401) 785-0400

Starting Point
P.O. Box 2277
Appleton, WI 54913-2277
(414) 735-5710

**Turning Point Career
Center—YWCA**
2600 Bancroft Way
Berkeley, CA 94704
(415) 848-6370

Wider Opportunities for Women
P.O. Box 35009
Charlotte, NC 28235
(704) 342-6532

Wider Opportunities for Women
1325 G Street NW, LL
Washington, DC 20005
(202) 638-3143

Women and Employment
601 Delaware Avenue
Charleston, WV 25302
(304) 345-1298

Women Employed Institute
22 West Monroe, Suite 1400
Chicago, IL 60603
(312) 782-3902

Women in Transition
1519 Clearlake Road
Cocoa, FL 32922
(407) 632-1111 x4600

Women's Job Counseling Center
34 Follen Street
Cambridge, MA 01238
(617) 547-1123

Women's Programs/Grays Harbor College
1620 Edward P. Smith Drive
Aberdeen, WA 98520
(206) 532-9020

Women's Vocational Services
Route 113, Box 548
Georgetown, DE 19947
(302) 856-5325

YWCA Transitional Services
P.O. Box 1667
Rock Springs, WY 82902
(307) 362-7923

MINORITY ORGANIZATIONS AND UNIVERSITIES

Alabama State University
Montgomery, AL 36195

Alcorn State University
Lorman, MS 39096

American Association of Black Women Entrepreneurs
P.O. Box 13933
Silver Spring, MD 20911-3933

Association of Black Sociologists
Virginia Commonwealth University
Richmond, VA 23284

Association of Corporate Professionals
7667 Maple Avenue, Suite 805
Takoma Park, MD 20012

Benedict College
Columbia, SC 29204

Bethune-Cookman College
Daytona Beach, FL 32015

Black Caucus/American Library Association
499 Wilson Library
Minneapolis, MN 55400

Black M.B.A. Association
234 5th Avenue
New York, NY 10001

Blacks in Government
1424 K Street NW—Suite 604
Washington, DC 20005

Central State University
Wilberforce, OH 45384

Chaflin College
Orangeburg, SC 29115

Cheyney State College
Cheyney, PA 19319

Coppin State College
Baltimore, MD 21216

Delaware State College
Dover, DE 19901

District of Columbia University
Washington, DC 20008

Fayetteville State University
Fayetteville, NC 28301

Howard University
Washington, DC 20059

Jackson State University
Jackson, MS 39217

Kentucky State University
Frankfort, KY 40601

Langston University
Langston, OK 73050

Lewis College of Business
Detroit, MI 48235

Lincoln University
Jefferson City, MO 65101

Lincoln University
Lincoln University, PA 19352

Minority Graduate Database
1515 U Street NW
Washington, DC 20009

Morehouse College
Atlanta, GA 30314

National Association/Black Social Workers
271 West 125th St., Suite 317
New York, NY 10027

National Association/Blacks in Criminal Justice
8121 Georgia Avenue, Suite 608
Silver Spring, MD 20910

National Bankers Association
122 C Street, Suite 580
Washington, DC 20001

National Dental Association
5506 Connecticut Ave. NW, Suite 24
Washington, DC 20015

National Pharmaceutical Association
2300 4th St. NW, College of Pharmacy
Washington, DC 20059

National Society of Black Engineers
Purdue University, CIVIL 1246
West Lafayette, IN 47907

Norfolk State University
Norfolk, VA 23504

Philander-Smith College
Little Rock, AR 72203

Savannah State College
Savannah, GA 31404

Southern University
Baton Rouge, LA 70813

Texas Southern University
Houston, TX 77004

Virginia State University
Petersburg, VA 23803

West Virginia State College
Institute, WV 25112

Xavier University
New Orleans, LA 70125

JOB TRAINING PARTNERSHIP AGENCIES

Department of Employment and Training
P.O. Box 488
Montpelier, VT 05602
(802) 229-0311

State JTPA Administrative Chief
101 Friendship Street
Providence, RI 02903
(401) 277-3930

State JTPA Administrator
John Fitch Plaza, Room 703-CN055
Trenton, NJ 08625
(609) 292-5005

State JTPA Administrator
700 Governors Drive
Pierre, SD 57501-2291
(605) 773-5017

State JTPA Contact
P.O. Box 2981
Little Rock, AR 72203
(501) 682-5227

State JTPA Director
P.O. Box 250347
Montgomery, AL 36125-0349
(205) 284-8800

State JTPA Director
P.O. Box 942880
Sacramento, CA 94280-0001
(916) 322-4440

State JTPA Director
720 S. Colorado Blvd., Suite 550
Denver, CO 80222
(303) 758-5020

State JTPA Director
200 Folly Brook Blvd.
Wethersfield, CT 06109
(203) 566-4290

State JTPA Director
P.O. Box 9499
Newark, DE 19714-9499
(302) 368-6810

State JTPA Director
500 C Street NW, Suite 600
Washington, DC 20001
(202) 639-1000

State JTPA Director
1320 Executive Center Dr., Suite 300
Tallahassee, FL 32399-0667
(904) 488-7228

State JTPA Director
148 International Blvd. NE, Suite 650
Atlanta, GA 30303
(404) 656-7392

State JTPA Director
830 Punchbowl Street, Room 316
Honolulu, HI 96813
(808) 548-6924

State JTPA Director
200 East Grand
Des Moines, IA 50309
(515) 242-4779

State JTPA Director
317 Main Street
Boise, ID 83735-0001
(208) 334-6131

State JTPA Director
620 East Adams Street
Springfield, IL 62701
(217) 785-6006

State JTPA Director
10 North Senate
Indianapolis, IN 46204
(317) 232-3270

State JTPA Director
401 S.W. Topeka Blvd.
Topeka, KS 66612
(913) 296-3588

State JTPA Director
275 E. Main St., 2 West
Frankfort, KY 40621
(502) 564-5360

State JTPA Director
P.O. Box 94094
Baton Rouge, LA 70804-9094
(504) 342-7620

State JTPA Director
19 Staniford St., 3rd Floor
Boston, MA 02114
(617) 727-6600

State JTPA Director
1100 N. Eutaw St., Suite 600
Baltimore, MD 21201
(301) 333-5070

State JTPA Director
State House Station 55
Augusta, ME 04333
(207) 289-3377

State JTPA Director
P.O. Box 30015
Lansing, MI 48909
(517) 373-9600

State JTPA Director
690 American Center Building
St. Paul, MN 55101
(612) 296-8008

State JTPA Director
P.O. Box 1087
Jefferson City, MO 65102-1087
(314) 751-4750

State JTPA Director
301 West Pearl Street
Jackson, MS 39203-3089
(601) 949-2234

State JTPA Director
P.O. Box 1728
Helena, MT 59624
(406) 444-4524

State JTPA Director
111 Seaboard Avenue
Raleigh, NC 27604
(919) 733-6383

State JTPA Director
P.O. Box 1537
Bismarck, ND 58502
(701) 224-2792

State JTPA Director
550 South 16th Street
Lincoln, NE 68509
(402) 471-2127

State JTPA Director
64B Old Suncook Road
Concord, NH 03301-5134
(603) 228-9500

State JTPA Director
P.O. Box 4218
Santa Fe, NM 87502
(505) 827-6827

State JTPA Director
400 W. King Street #108
Carson City, NV 89710
(702) 687-4310

State JTPA Director
State Office Building Campus,
Building 12
Albany, NY 12240-0250
(518) 457-4317

State JTPA Director
P.O. Box 1618
Columbus, OH 43216
(614) 466-3817

State JTPA Director
201 Will Rogers Building
Oklahoma City, OK 73105
(405) 557-7200

State JTPA Director
775 Summer Street NE
Salem, OR 97310
(503) 373-1995

State JTPA Director
7th and Forster Sts., Room 1700
Harrisburg, PA 17120
(717) 787-1745

State JTPA Director
P.O. Box 995
Columbia, SC 29202
(803) 737-2400

State JTPA Director
501 Union Building, 6th Floor
Nashville, TN 37243-0658
(615) 741-1031

State JTPA Director
P.O. Box 12728
Austin, TX 78711
(512) 834-6106

State JTPA Director
324 S. State, Suite 210
Salt Lake City, UT 84111
(801) 538-8750

State JTPA Director
4615 W. Broad Street
Richmond, VA 23230
(804) 367-9800

State JTPA Director
212 Maple Park, Mail Stop KG-11
Olympia, WA 98504-5311
(206) 753-5149

State JTPA Director
P.O. Box 7972
Madison, WI 53707
(608) 266-2439

State JTPA Director
112 California Ave., Room 211
Charleston, WV 25305
(304) 348-5920

State JTPA Director
P.O. Box 2760
Casper, WY 82604
(307) 235-3601

State JTPA Program Administrator
P.O. Box 6123, Site Code:920 Z
Phoenix, AZ 85005
(602) 542-3957

State JTPA Program Manager
949 E. 36th Ave., Suite 400
Anchorage, AK 99508
(907) 563-1955

MILITARY PROGRAMS

Army Career/Alumni Program
2461 Eisenhower Ave.
Alexandria, VA 22331-0479
(703) 325-3591

U.S. Army ROTC Cadet Command
ATTN: ATCC-MP
Fort Monroe, VA 23651

Veterans Employment/Training Service
200 Constitution Ave. NW
Washington, DC 20210

RECRUITMENT DATABASES

Career Placement Registry
302 Swann Avenue
Alexandria, VA 22301
(800) 368-3093/(703) 683-1085
(in VA)

College Recruitment Database
9585 Valparaiso Court
Indianapolis, IN 46268
(317) 872-2045

CORS: Sales Department
1 Pierce Place, Suite 300 E
Itasca, IL 60143
(800) 323-1352

First Interview
5500 Interstate N. Pkwy. #425
Atlanta, GA 30328
(404) 952-1058

JOBSource
1720 W. Mulberry St. #89
Fort Collins, CO 80521-3362
(303) 493-1779

Korn/Ferry International
600 Montgomery St., 31st Floor
San Francisco, CA 94111
(415) 956-1834

Minority Graduate Database
1515 U Street NW
Washington, DC 20009

National Insurance Recruiters Association
P.O. Box 7811
Marietta, GA 30065-7811
(404) 565-5213

Résumés on Computer
1000 Waterway Blvd.
Indianapolis, IN 46202
(317) 636-1000

Texas Savings & Loan League
408 West 14th Street
Austin, TX 78701
(512) 476-6131

The Executives Network
160 State Street
Boston, MA 02109
(617) 227-3784

University ProNet Inc.
3803 E. Bayshore Rd. #150
Palo Alto, CA 94303
(415) 691-1600

Index

About the Author

Catherine D. Fyock, SPHR, is president of Innovative Management Concepts, a Lousiville, Kentucky management firm specializing in creative strategies to recruit and retain employees. She is noted for her work in the employment of nontraditional labor market segments, including the older worker.

Some of her clients include Hardee's Food Systems, AT&T, Federal Express, the National Restaurant Association, the National Retail Federation, and the Society for Human Resource Management.

An often-quoted authority in her field, she is also a noted lecturer, seminar leader, and author whose articles on employment issues have appeared widely in both professional and trade publications. She is also the author of *America's Work Force Is Coming of Age: What Every Business Needs to Know to Recruit, Train, Manage, and Retain an Aging Work Force* (Lexington Books/Macmillan Inc.).

For further information on services provided by Innovative Management Concepts, contact Catherine Fyock at P.O. Box 1229, Crestwood, Ky 40014, telephone: 502-228-3869, 1-800-277-0384.